"Leeana's words have taught me how to ___

    —**Myquillyn Smith**, The Nester, author of *The Nesting Place*

"We all want to find our voice, feel comfortable in our own skin, and come out of hiding. Leeana is a trustworthy companion on this journey of becoming broken and beautiful."

    —**Rebekah Lyons**, author of *Freefall to Fly*

"Leeana Tankersley has the gift of breathing life into the weary souls of women; souls exhausted from anxiety, from negative self-talk and unfulfilled dreams. Leeana sees those souls and puts her arms around them, breathes life back into them through prophetic verse and gentle, pragmatic exercise. She draws the wounded daughter back into the lap of her heavenly Father, and invites her home."

    —**Emily T. Wierenga**, founder of The Lulu Tree
    and author of *Atlas Girl* and *Making It Home*

"If you ever feel inclined to apologize for your own existence in this world, then please, *please* read this insightful, soulful book. A writer with as much spice and sass as compassion and grace, Leeana is the friend providing you with peace in your personhood as she shows you how to see yourself as your Creator does. This book will unhook you from your false press as it anchors you to your true identity: You are a brazen and beloved creation worth celebrating."

    —**Kristen Strong**, author of *Girl Meets Change:*
    Truths to Carry You through Life's Transitions

Praise for *Breathing Room*

"Leeana refuses to reach for easy answers, instead leading the reader on a journey of accepting our own humanity. Quite simply, this is one of the most thoughtful books I've read all year."

—**Emily P. Freeman**, author of *A Million Little Ways*

"Leeana says out loud the things we all feel, and she says it with grace and eloquence. Reading these pages is like sitting with a friend."

—**Shauna Niequist**, author of *Bread & Wine*

"A new lyrical voice in a crowded world, Tankersley tells a tale of hope, reality, and everything in between."

—**Claire Díaz-Ortiz**, author, speaker, and innovator at Twitter, Inc.

"Tankersley sparkles as she creates melodious prose in her new book, *Breathing Room*. Her ability to take a simple 'let go and let God' message and weave it into her own journey through frustration, anger, despair, discovery, and ultimately triumph is enticing. Her beautifully worded short stories punctuate a message that every woman regardless of age faced at least once in her life. This title is perfect for frustrated mothers or anyone who is discouraged with life and ready to take the first step and read the story of a fellow sojourner in life."

—*CBA Retailers+Resources*

Brazen

The Courage to Find the You That's Been Hiding

LEEANA TANKERSLEY

Revell

a division of Baker Publishing Group
Grand Rapids, Michigan

© 2016 by Leeana Tankersley

Published by Revell
a division of Baker Publishing Group
PO Box 6287, Grand Rapids, MI 49516-6287
www.revellbooks.com

Printed in the United States of America

Library of Congress Cataloging-in-Publication Data
Names: Tankersley, Leeana, 1975– author.
Title: Brazen : the courage to find the you that's been hiding / Leeana Tankersley.
Description: Grand Rapids, MI : Revell Books, 2016. | Includes bibliographical references.
Identifiers: LCCN 2015044000 | ISBN 9780800726829 (pbk.)
Subjects: LCSH: Self-actualization (Psychology)—Religious aspects—Christianity. | Self-actualization (Psychology) in women. | Integrity—Religious aspects—Christianity. | Christian women—Religious life.
Classification: LCC BV4598.2 .T36 2016 | DDC 248.4—dc23 LC record available at http://lccn.loc.gov/2015044000

Author is represented by Christopher Ferebee, Attorney and Literary Agent, www.christopherferebee.com

16 17 18 19 20 21 22   7 6 5 4 3 2 1

To Laura, who is brazen

Contents

Contents

Contents

Note to Reader

If you were attending one of my workshops—where we spend three hours focused entirely on reflection and expression—I would tell you that these practices of reflection and expression will heal you, enliven you, return you to yourself, create space for God to speak to you, and therefore bring you home.

So when it came time to write a book about coming out of hiding, I could not help but include an opportunity for you to engage in the lifelines of reflection and expression for yourself. These two movements—like inhaling and exhaling—are literal soul sustenance. And I didn't want you to miss out on that spectacular opportunity.

To that end, I've included prompts at the conclusion of each chapter that will help you interact with the material. Sorry if this feels presumptuous, annoying, or overly aggressive.

But if by chance these prompts feel like an invitation—even if that invitation is a bit uncomfortable—I'm right here, cheering you on, believing that examining your inner landscape will pay off big time and that getting your hands moving will always help heal your mind. Oh, and grabbing a couple of friends and talking through your findings could be (and I don't want to overemphasize this, of course) life-changing.

If you do the prompts, I hereby affirm the employment of "legal bribes" to yourself. You, Brazen Warrior, get to reward yourself with something delicious, frivolous, or otherwise longed for. Might I suggest a metallic Sharpie. Or a coconut La Croix. Maybe a fresh new journal. Or a walk in the woods.

Let's call it positive reinforcement.

You might also want to invest in a candle you love that you could light and enjoy when you are doing your Brazen Work. And, I don't want this to come across bossy in any way, but I think scouting out a little nook in your house or out in the world that could be the place where you go to reflect and express would be supremely helpful.

What we want to do is set up an environment that is so warm and friendly and safe and nurturing that our souls can't help but come out and play. For some of us, the most sacred parts of us have been in hiding for too long, and we need to create a place where we are just comfortable enough to emerge.

In addition to the prompts at the end of each chapter, you will see suggestions for building a Brazen Board. Think of it as a storyboard for your soul.

You are going to collect images, ideas, and words that we'll combine—throughout the book—to create a Brazen Board, a physical manifestation of the ways in which you want to exercise your brazen.

If you decide to create a board, it will be helpful to have some of the following on hand: poster board (or some kind of canvas), glue stick or rubber cement, scissors, magazines or any kind of visually stimulating papers, cards, images. As you are reading, keep your eye out for anything found that speaks to you in your daily life—shells, leaves, keys, dried petals, colors, textures, an old photograph, you name it. You might also want markers, Mod Podge, or paints.

You can make this project as sophisticated or as simple as you'd like. There are no rules, and you do not need to feel the pressure to Martha Stewart it to death. Let your board be a process, a prayer, more than a product.

I have found that sometimes we need help exploring our own soul, nurturing our voice, remembering our identity. And these interactive elements can help us access what has gone dormant.

But not if you feel like punching me in the face upon the mention of these exercises. In that case, certainly, just keep movin' right along.

Part One

Receive

{YOUR IDENTITY}

1

Honor Your Created Center

When they heard the sound of GOD strolling in the garden in the evening breeze, the Man and his Wife hid in the trees of the garden, hid from GOD. *GOD called to the Man: "Where are you?"* He said, "I heard you in the garden and I was afraid because I was naked. And I hid."

—Genesis 3:8–10 Message (emphasis added)

I sat on my back patio very late at night, after everyone else was in bed, and I scribbled on a legal pad. Through the palm trees around our patio, I could see lights from the city beyond our house. Every once in a while I would look up so I could take in the visual spaciousness I was longing for internally.

I wanted to start a couple of new creative projects. In fact, the persistent desire for self-expression was working itself into a lather inside my soul. I could feel the energy behind it, because creative self-expression is a language formed by

God in eternity itself, a language I love, so it whispers to the very core of me.

But the Soul Bullies—those bullies who are in hot pursuit of my freedom—would have none of it, and they started in with their old stories about me: how I get myself into messes, how I can't be content, how I'm not someone who can be happy, how I'll regret my creative decisions. The Soul Bullies are the ancestors of that insipid garden snake, slithering around me until they turn me upside down and inside out and shake the treasure right out of me. They scare me off, rattle me to the point that I no longer have any idea who I'm supposed to be listening to. What is God's voice? What is my soul voice? What is the bully's voice?

Commence the tangle.

On the night of the back patio session, the tangle was taking over, so I did what I do now, what I've learned—the hard way—I must do when I'm in these scrapes. I set my phone timer for twenty minutes and listen with deep compassion to myself instead of jumping right to judging, overriding, denying. Instead of assuming the longing is coming from an untrustworthy source, I simply give myself permission to listen.

Immediately I hear the following two sentences of doom:

1. How dare you.

and

2. Who do you think you are?

If I really take a minute to consider the source of these two sentences, I realize they are the mantras of fear and shame. They are the calling cards of the Soul Bully. But, when my soul is cornered by these convincing lies, I can't quite discern their origin. They hiss:

How dare you dabble.

How dare you romp, frolic, play.

How dare you desire.

How dare you try and fail.

How dare you follow an inkling.

How dare you believe in yourself.

How dare you trust your perceptions.

How dare you see yourself as a reliable observer of this world.

How dare you go big.

How dare you speak up.

How dare you let your gorgeousness off the leash.

How dare you sing.

How dare you paint.

How dare you write.

How dare you make magic.

How dare you love what you offer this world.

How dare you feel fabulous in your own skin.

How dare you take a single step without having it all figured out first.

How dare you let anyone see your holy and holey humanity.

How dare you not know.

How dare you learn the hard way.

How dare you believe any of this matters anyway.

How dare you say how you really feel.

How dare you create a boundary.

How dare you clear space for yourself.

How dare you announce your arrival.

How dare you feel entitled to your own soul.

How dare you don a bold lip and a statement necklace.

"Who. Do. You. Think. You. Are?" And then he finishes me off with the sucker punch, "I'll tell you who you are. You, Leeana, are the world's biggest imposter."

I'm tired of fighting. I'm tired of pushing back against them and their attempts to disconnect me from myself. Their entire agenda is to convince me I'll be better off if I abandon the pure gold in my gut. The problem with this is that every time I do, every time I decide I'll just give up or settle or let go of the longings, I end up feeling like an actor in my own life. I feel like I've lost myself, like I don't know for sure who I am anymore, like the best parts of me are hiding. And it's no good. In fact, it's soul death.

Do you ever feel like this? Something true inside you is trying to emerge—pressing up from the depths—but because it feels sacred and mysterious and wildly free and therefore gloriously dangerous, some dark and tormenting Soul Bully is immediately on your case. A desire, whisper, longing, stirring is welling up, but so is fear, so is an unnerving anxiety. A bully is lurking, and you find yourself in what could best be described as a soul tug-of-war. You find yourself skeptical of you.

This is basically the story of my entire life. Or at least it feels that way some days. I want to follow this voice, this beat, the creative itch in my hands and heart, but something, or someone, is invested in keeping her quiet. Keeping her small. Keeping her confused. Keeping her confined. Keeping her paralyzed. Someone is trying to talk me out of living from my Created Center.

Many theological giants have described this "Created Center" I'm talking about. Henri Nouwen identifies it as the "divinely endowed center." Thomas Merton calls it "the God-given center of our being," St. Augustine writes about "the divine center," and John Calvin terms it "the divine spark." Some call it the true self or our essential identity, the image-bearing part of you, your spirit, or your soul. I believe this untouchable place inside you is the part of your being where God himself put his hands in the wet concrete of your existence and said, "You are formed in my image" and "It is good."

Not only is it good. It is God-in-you good. It is the part of you that longs for truth, beauty, breath, home, love. It is the part of you that notices sunsets and holds a baby close to smell his neck and longs to rescue those who do not know freedom. It is the part of you that sees with eternal eyes and feels with divine intuition. It is the part of you that is both complete *and* becoming. It is the you and the me that is fiercely free.

Where is she?

Some people would have you believe you are inherently, essentially flawed because of your sin and your humanity. My deepest conviction, and the basis for this entire writing, is the opposite: that underneath all of the parts of us that are wrecked and wounded and flawed and human is God-in-us. Our essential God-image. And while we will never be perfect—we will never be God—one of our greatest temptations in life is to believe that the God-image is not enough, and one of our greatest longings in life is to live from what we already, deep-down know . . . that, in fact, the God-image stamped in our souls is more than enough. It is everything.

In *A God to Call Father*, Michael Phillips writes, "Goodness lies deeper in the heart of man's nature than sin, which came later and entered from the outside. Goodness lies deeper in man because God put himself there. It was very good! Goodness is intrinsic to man's nature; sin is not. Sin is the corrupting virus that has temporarily corrupted goodness."[1]

Do I believe God put something good inside me on the day of creation that I am to investigate, nurture, return to? Or do I believe the Soul Bullies—that I am a fraud and a fake and a fool for thinking I am entitled to the eternity God set in my heart?[2] Could I change the course of human history each morning by waking up and choosing to honor the Created Center inside me instead of abandon her? This is the most courageous work. And. I'm. Ready.

I'm writing this book at age thirty-nine, just a couple of months away from crossing over into a new decade, and this threshold has my attention like none other. I feel a little scrappy, like I'm ready to pick a fight. On the defeated days, I want a do-over on my thirties, a chance to go back and be the more brazen version of myself. I want redemption for all the days I was sad and tired and recovering and barely breathing. Once again, this is the voice of the Soul Bullies who are always telling me it's too late and that I'll be stuck forever. This is the voice telling me I cannot trust the process, that things will always feel the way they do right now, which are two of the biggest lies we're told.

On the days when I'm clearer, I see that it has all—and I mean ALL—led me to this moment. Nothing is wasted. I peer over the fence, looking at the next decade, and I push up my sleeves.

What would it be like to try something completely different on this threshold of eras? What if, instead of trying to outrun the Soul Bullies and their lies, I simply stopped, sat down, and—in the presence of my Maker—returned to the Created Center in me. Asked him to show me the way *home* instead of letting the Soul Bullies convince me to *hide*?

Could these words from the incomparable Maya Angelou be the battle cry rising up from my Created Center, "Your crown has been bought and paid for. Put it on your head and wear it."[3]

So I go to the patio, I confront the serpentine "How dare you" and "Who do you think you are?"

Because no matter how many times I tell the Soul Bullies to go away, they come slithering back around. No matter how many times I welcome them and sit them down and tell them they're not in charge, they start hissing louder than all the other voices. So I had to begin again with the reality that my soul has legitimate longings I need to listen to and that the bullies want to scare off all the really good, God-designed beauty living in my being.

Talking about our souls, our dreams, our desires, our longings can seem very romantic. Excruciatingly romantic. I have talked about these things as if they were pedicures and bubble baths. What I'm realizing is that these soul pursuits require guts. Blood and guts. Because every dark force in the world wants to keep us from exploring our God-given wild.

The garden snake convinced us that what we had already been given was not enough. We must seek out something more or different, because what was created in us and for us will not satisfy.

So we grabbed for more, forged ahead of the plan, tried to secure our own sense of self. And it did not produce. Then we ran for cover. We hid because we weren't sure who to trust anymore, especially whether or not we could trust ourselves.

I sat on that back patio for far longer than twenty minutes, to tell you the truth. Maybe ninety. Maybe more. I couldn't quit the inky sky and the breeze. I didn't want to short-circuit the sacred moment. I didn't want to move, actually. In the way that you don't want to scare off the most intrepid butterfly that has somehow come to light on your shoulder. Or in the way that you don't want to get out from underneath your coziest blanket on a crisp morning.

What presented itself was not so much a solution but an encounter, which is its own kind of solution, I guess. Treading into eternity can, ironically, help us become much more present to what's happening right here, what's happening right now. In a matter of ninety back-patio moments, I felt a shift. There I was . . . *me catching up with me* . . . realizing, once again, something eternal lives and breathes in me, and it is good. God-given good.

Some days I crumble under the weight of the Soul Bully's finger wagging. Not today. Today, I'm armed with my legal pad and my phone timer. I write out each of these sentences. One by hideous one. I look at them. I make eye contact with the venom.

This is a good thing to do regularly. Look all that crap right in the eye and see if it holds. See if it really, actually holds. See if these words are anything God would ever come close to saying to us, dear daughters. Our blind belief in lies is the greatest enemy of our God-given wild. When you put the lies in front of you, you start to see how grotesquely overrated shame is. It's hot air, but it burns if we breathe it in.

I'd like to tell you that at this point in my life I'm done with all that. I'm done believing all the very things that will hurt me most. I'm done walking hand in hand with fear and shame. I'm done giving them the power. The truth is, I don't have that kind of control. I am not God. So, because I can't cure myself of these hot-breathed Soul Bullies, I have to learn how to trick them. And one of the most interesting and exciting ways I know to trick these bullies is by getting to know my soul a bit more intimately. In the presence of my soul's Maker.

The day after my time on the patio, my daughter Lane has found my legal pad. On every page she has gone through and written "I Luve You Mom" and "I Luve You." She's written over the top of my words, my musings, my stirrings, my notes—none of which she can really decipher yet. "I Luve You" in her six-year-old-magic printing that includes a little heart here and a curly swirl there. This recurring note reduces me further and further with every page I turn. It's her big, looping letters written across my own hurried handwriting, my own restless scratchings, the how dare you insults, and the who do you think you are accusations. I feel like I might fall down dead, it is so tender. I'm given a visual manifestation of my previous evening's dabble into eternity, where this wild, looping love meets all my longings. I'm reminded <u>love covers us</u>.

I'm tired of the story of deception, shame, hiding. I'm ready for a different cycle, a new trajectory. It is time. Time to reach down into the annals of your being and explore all the dimensions of who and what God knit there. It is time to come out of hiding. Let's go after what's been silenced, hidden, lost, bruised, abused, abandoned, bullied. Let's do it together, sisters, linking arms and heading into the fray.

"Leeana," he says to me, and he says to you, like he did to those first humans so long ago, "where are you?"

This book is an exploration of that question.

Reflection & Expression

What is one persistent longing you carry?

For Your Brazen Board

Collage or write the words "My Created Center" or "My Inner Brazen" or "My God-Given Wild."

2

Emerge from the Beige

"Here I am between my flock and my treasure," the boy thought.

He had to choose between something he had become accustomed to and something he wanted to have.

—Paulo Coelho, *The Alchemist*

The word *brazen* swam up from my soul and out of my mouth, intuitively, a few years ago. We were living in the desert of the Middle East, stationed there for my husband Steve's job in the Navy. At that time in my life, my interior landscape matched the Middle Eastern landscape: beige. The sky was beige. The sand was beige. The buildings were beige. This is how I felt on the inside too. A million miles away from home, taking care of babies in a foreign and volatile world, slightly traumatized and definitely hypervigilant from a massive move and the—hardly worth mentioning—civil infighting going on around us.

You have likely been through a season like this. Not the beige of the Middle East, of course, but a beige all your own—a season of infighting, a season of trauma, a season of displacement and disorientation. The light has become flat. A dimension seems to be missing. Breathing is about as much as can be accomplished in a day.

During those beige days, I saw something that woke me for a second, in a subversive way. I was stopped on a dirt road near our villa. My eyes wandered out the window. Gutter water ran beside my car, and riding high on the tide were the most striking hot pink bougainvillea petals dancing along. I whispered audibly, like a murmur from beyond, "*Brazen*."

The word *brazen* isn't necessarily part of my everyday lexicon. In fact, I don't remember ever saying it out loud before that moment. So it kind of surprised me when it spilled out of my mouth. It also delighted me, because I agree with what C. S. Lewis wrote in his novel *Till We Have Faces*: "To say the very thing you really mean, the whole of it, nothing more or less or other than what you really mean; that's the whole art and joy of words."[1] And I nailed it.

The dictionary definition of *brazen* is this perfect phrase: *without shame*. And it goes on from there: unrestrained by convention or propriety. Nervy. Bold-faced. Audacious. Shameless. Brazen has traditionally been forced into the arms of the word *hussy*—as in, "Wow, she's a brazen hussy"—which is, as you might imagine, less than complimentary. Brazen needs to be rescued from the clutches of hussy and delivered into the hands of holy, because it's a word worth using, a word worth living, without hussy following it around.

In that dull sludge water, I saw my own longing reflected back to me, my longing to feel that beautiful pink instead of all the beige, all the sludgy gutter water. I wanted the color back. I wanted to feel freedom to do and be and dance and play. Freedom to roam and risk and create and work. Freedom to love and rest and taste and see. Freedom to make and believe and dream and fight. Freedom to speak up and speak out and to know what it is I want to say. But instead, the beige sky and the brown gutter water so entirely overwhelmed any pink that wanted to emerge.

I have a jumpy, busy mind and a nervous, buzzy body that walk around with me every day. I spend a lot of time taking care of this body and this mind. Some days are good days and I feel like I'm on top of my game. Some days, the Hard days, I'm so tired of standing up to them, babying them, working with them, working around them.

Some days I feel like my issues and my identity are one and the same. I believe I am fatally flawed, and I will never be free. The weight of this lie all but buries me. It makes me angry, rage-y, because I am so entirely tired of being tired. I want peace.

Recently I sat with a trusted guide and told her how angry I was that I couldn't just take a pill or make an appointment and solve my issues once and for all. "I do both those things," I tell her, "and they don't seem to be fixing me. I work really hard to take care of myself, to take care of all the buzzing and busy, but I'm not making any progress."

She looked at me and said, "Leeana, you must believe me when I tell you that you are not where you were. You have learned to take care of yourself, love yourself through the Hard days, turn toward help, let God in. You are not where you were."

I was talking with the most stunning twentysomething the other day. She told me about the ongoing sexual abuse she experienced in her home. She told me about how she fled, and how she fears that no matter what she does, she will always be defined by the abuse.

When I look at her and listen to her, I see this extraordinary soul—someone who is getting herself the help she needs, investing in her own healing and recovery, taking herself out into nature to ingest beauty, putting on mascara.

28

Her insides feel raw and traumatized and overwhelmed. But what I see when I look at her and hear her story is pure, unmitigated resilience. *She is doing it.* She is showing up. She is living. The waters of her life have been as dirty and disgusting as one could imagine. Undoubtedly, life would feel so much simpler to just give in to the beige constantly looming all around her. And yet there she is, as hot pink as she could be, even in the midst of all that sludge. She still feels buried, like the power of it all will never lift, but I want to say to her with conviction, "You are not where you were. You are moving through this. Slowly, painfully, indirectly. You have to believe, *you are not where you were.*"

I am so often waiting for all the Hard to dissipate before I believe I can really live. But perhaps the solution isn't the absence of the Hard, it's what we do when we're in the midst of it. Will we succumb to colorless, motionless, woefulness, martyrdom? Or will we persevere, look for the hope?

Sometimes, for a season, all we can expect from ourselves is to sit on the floor and breathe. And that's plenty. But then, after a week or a month or a year or three, after we have caught our breath, we must do the work of remembering that our issues are not the same thing as our identity. We must emerge.

Walking into living color is vulnerable. So very vulnerable. It's like coming out from a dark room and you have to squint to tolerate the light. But at some point we have to consider the truth Eep Crood already told us when she said, "Dad, not dying isn't the same thing as living."[2] We let our eyes open again. We let our hearts and souls wake up instead of believing that life and faith and healing and recovery are one big trick.

We do the brazen work of going after the "you" and the "me" that's been hiding, buried, muted, lost, abandoned. We invest in our own healing. We do it as a debt of honor to ourselves and as our most profound worship to God, our Creator. We will not live in the dark, even if that means we have to walk around squinting for a time. We will let ourselves be seen. We will let ourselves be free. We will emerge.

There is no perfect time to be courageous. Our emergence doesn't happen when we are at our most brave. It often happens when we are at our most bruised. We choose to lean into the tears and the fears and the dreams and the wild and we decide we will not hide. Even though hiding feels like so much less work.

What if you and I are stronger than we think, are more intuitive than we assume, possess greater competence than we'll admit, have more of a voice than we believe? When you and I question our strength, our tenacity, our perseverance, our butt-kicking potential, let's remember one seriously outrageous fact:

God himself gave us dominion. He entrusted us with influence, responsibility, and authority. He gave us charge. He put us on this planet and said, "Here you go. Enjoy. Work your magic." He literally gave us a world and gave us the right and privilege of naming everything in it. He gave us creative work. He also gave us the capacity to delight in what we see, hear, smell, taste. He did that because he knew, better than we did, about the Created Center within us. The shameless center that is Other.

I want to explore with all the license of a poet. I want to experience with all the authority of a child. I want to express with all the abandon of one who has been given an endless palate to play with. My wanderlusting soul longs for this walkabout through creation. And he says, "It is yours. Go. Dabble. Remember who you are."

You are not abuse. You are not anxiety. You are not depression. You are not infertility. You are not divorce. You are not abortion. You are not addiction. You are not failure. You are not your body. You are not the beige. You are the beloved, precious soul. The brazen, beautiful beloved.

So many of us have lived with any number of things that have gnawed into the longed-for freedom. Mind plagues. Pesky habits with the forbidden. The worst kind of worry. A tendency to shrink. A timid tongue. Harsh accusers. Mean people. A total lack of confidence in a bathing suit. And so on. We begin to believe that the power of these issues exceeds the power of our identity. We lose track of our own resilience, the creative strength God himself put within us.

And then we take one look into the eyes of the most fragile victim and see a junkyard dog within her who is gloriously fighting for herself. Imperfectly. Irreverently. Impossibly. Fighting. Emerging, one just-perceptible step at a time, eyes still adjusting to the light, in all her brazen glory.

Hot pink riding high on gutter water. The kind of in-your-face pink that reminds me of the Holi celebration in India. I'm kind of obsessed with Holi, the ancient Hindu festival of color. Participants usher in the end of winter and the arrival of spring with a "celebration of colors," chasing each other through the streets with spray bottles and homemade powders until every inch of every person is covered in the most impossibly vibrant colors. No one is too young or too old. No one is off limits. The effect, captured in extraordinary images, will take your breath away. The festival is said to be a celebration signifying the victory of good over evil. When I look at pictures of the Holi festival, I cannot help but feel the exuberance, the vibrancy, the saturation, and it calls to my Unashamed Center, awakening the very best parts of me to life in living color.

Reflection & Expression

The etymology of *brazen* tells us the word comes from the same word meaning brass. But, to me, the color of brazen is the hot pink of those bougainvillea petals.

If you were to close your eyes and think of something brazen, what color would it be? The color does not have to be your favorite one, necessarily, though it might be. What matters most is that the color stirs something sacred in you. If you're still not sure, here are a few other questions to ask yourself:

> What is the color of your soul, your Created Center?
> What is the color you associate with freedom?
> What is the color you think of when you think of the word *alive*?

Begin collecting images and items in that color. Stockpile everything you can in your color. Let yourself be drawn to it. Spend some time writing about your color, even if it's just a few minutes. Keep your pen moving. Answer the prompt: Why am I drawn to this color? What does it mean to me?

For Your Brazen Board

Choose some of the images you've curated in your color. You could also splash some paint onto your board or paint your hand and make a handprint in your color. Choose a pen in your color and write a word or two on your board, perhaps taking those words from the writing you did above. Whatever you decide to include, let your intuition guide you as you select words and images, beginning a dialogue with your soul voice.

3

Take Twenty Minutes of Soul Time

If she got really quiet and listened, new parts of her wanted to speak.

—Susan Ariel

I am a firm believer in guides—people who can take us by the hand and lead us one step further down the path, one pass deeper into our story, one beat closer to our truth. These are the people who can help coax our inner brazen out of hiding. Guides can fall into a number of categories: therapists, pastors, coaches, children, teachers, mentors, and more. One of my guides is a spiritual director named Beth. I see her once a month and I never see her that I don't end up in tears, one way or another. She's some kind of angel with dreads, and—as a spiritual director does—she listens and looks for God in my story and points me back to his tide of love and healing in my life, all the while keeping a wary eye on my soul for even the faintest whiff of the Soul Bullies. What a gift.

Beth-with-Dreads encouraged me to start a new practice that has now become what you might call "unforced rhythms of grace" in my life.[1] She told me to start spending twenty minutes with my soul as often as I could.

I hate to admit it, but I have distrusted this kind of thing most of my life. I've distrusted that I could sustain such a discipline or that it would even make any kind of difference. I wondered if these practices were about earning something, which left them hollow. So, I sabotaged myself a hundred thousand different ways, believing I could get what I wanted and needed if I just tried a little harder: analyzed a little more, thought about it all longer.

But when we don't take the time to listen, we dis-integrate. We are walking heads. We're trying to think our way *around* the tangle instead of listening our way *through*.

It's hard work to discern the soul stirrings, to quiet down and just listen without evaluating the veracity or usefulness or practicality of what's emerging from the depths. In the short run, living from the neck up is so much easier. Until it isn't . . .

The tangle inside us needs unraveling. And after we've convinced ourselves that running as fast as we can will undo the knot, we somehow realize it's only making the knot tighter.

I can fall back on being a "try-er" by nature. Someone who muscles through. Once I've tried and tried and tried, then I find I'm so tired. Funny how *tried* and *tired* are practically the same word if you look at them side by side.

By "try" here, I mean the frantic strive, hustle, press. I'm not saying some endeavors in life aren't difficult, challenging, requiring work. But work is different from that endless try. Work has a destination. Try is a treadmill.

When all our effort runs out, when all our chasing is exhausted, when all our solving proves futile, when all our analysis is in vain . . . then, and only then, do we happen upon a space where we are totally quiet before God. I wonder if this is where he wanted us all along. Perhaps all God wants is to get us still enough so he can pat our arm gently and say, "Shh, it's OK. Shh. I'm here." This is grace, and it trumps our try every single day of the week.

Few things have taught me about grace—and it's unforced-ness—like the practice of twenty minutes of soul time. Making space to get really quiet and listen is holy work. And it's kind of crazy what emerges if we'll stop striving and just surrender. We receive God afresh. We happen upon the God-in-us inter-section and we are gifted with a sustaining encounter. I believe encounters reveal what our efforts never could.

I take my legal pad out to the courtyard at the front of our house, and I turn on the fountain and position a folding chair by a pretty aqua pot with—you guessed it—bougainvillea. I smell the jasmine overgrowing the gate down below the courtyard, feel the wind, and hear the music created by the movement in the palm fronds. I turn my face toward the sun, the warmth and light.

Just this—walking outside and breathing in the world, if we will make time to do it—is intoxicating. I had spent a good portion of the last two years indoors, which was due to a num-ber of factors, including work, mental health, and my energy level. It was now time to receive the aliveness of the world and be energized by its essence.

I take a couple of deep breaths as a means of finding my way back to my body. I can so easily be floating outside my own ex-istence, and this practice is an opportunity to find my way back to myself. So I breathe and try to settle down into my seat, and I listen to whatever is stirring up in my soul. What am I afraid of? What anxieties am I carrying? What am I worried about? Where does my body hurt? What longings are lurking? What angst is making me crazy? What tension am I experiencing? Any feelings that have energy behind them get recorded. Again, I'm not trying to make sense of anything. I'm simply showing up, keeping my pen moving, trying to take notes for my soul.

After about ten to fifteen minutes of soul-recording, I write, *God, what do you want to say to me about all this?*

This step is so important because it formally invites God into my tangles. Of course he's already there, already waiting for me, but I need to be reminded of that fact, reminded that he wants to offer wisdom, comfort, love, truth. So I ask him what he wants to tell me, and then I listen and write, listen and write. I do all this until my phone timer chimes.

Here's the linchpin: I ask God to help me let go and embrace the flow of what surfaces, instead of judging, analyzing, evaluating the contents of my soul and his responses. For those twenty minutes, I'm not allowed to be a soul skeptic. I'm not allowed to reach for holds. I am to submit to the tide.

This summer I took my kids up to Tahoe to visit my in-laws. One morning we ventured out to the Yuba River with our clunky water shoes and coolers and giant tubes. The Clampetts go to Tahoe. The water was so clear you could see down to the river floor, and despite the drought here in California, the water ran just fast enough that we could catch a ride. We took turns escorting the littlest cousins, Ollie and Elle, down the river while the big kids drank grape soda on the shore. After a couple of attempts, we were all learning how to best maneuver our tubes between rocks, other tubers, the minor-league rapids. My son Luke said it best after his first run: "Well, there's one thing I've learned already: Don't fight the river."

Yes. This is the image we are to take with us into our twenty minutes of soul time. We are to trust the flow.

Here's how I started: feeling slightly desperate for a new way, ready to stop hiding and trying, and ready for more love and trusting. I believed that the only way *out* is always *through*. I ordered a thing or two on Amazon to help seal the deal. I found a pen that spoke to me and a place that nurtured me. I lit a candle some days, a fire in the fireplace others. I made an almond milk latte. I set a timer for twenty minutes. And I listened. Wrote. Listened. Wrote.

And then I did it again. And a few days later, I did it again. An unforced rhythm of grace.

That's it.

Sitting down and listening is not necessarily revolutionary in theory. But it is revolutionary in practice. As an extrovert with a busy brain, I find it almost embarrassingly obvious that I would need to sit down and be still. So obvious, in fact, that I don't do it. And then my brain gets busier and my body gets buzzier, and the next thing you know I've dis-integrated, and I'm a head walking around with lots of ideas and lots of plans and lots of solutions . . . and no soul.

No one—including my kids, my husband, my friends, or God—benefits from this version of me. Sure, they will love me even when I'm in this state, but I am not the me I was created to be. And therefore, *I* suffer in this equation too, because I am completely disconnected from the Source. As we listen to ourselves, we create space for God. And as we encounter God, we find ourselves.

I think every one of us is longing for an encounter with God. For something true that intersects with our real lives and our real needs. We long to not just study about him, but to meet with him. And, even more, to meet with him in a way that has bearing on what is actually going on in our own lives. To hear him speaking over us. To feel him reaching toward us.

Your soul, your Created Center, is where all of you and all of God dwells. You don't analyze, think, or study your way there. You push the urgent back and you sit and you listen. You come to a point where you realize the rest of your life isn't going to work if this twenty minutes doesn't happen regularly. It's a recalibration. It's a reintegration. In those twenty minutes, allow yourself to be met with grace. Again, this isn't about you working your way to God. This is about you sitting down long enough for God to get to you.

Desires will surface. Memories will walk right toward you. You might see yourself as a child. You might remember a dream you hadn't thought about in years. You might think of something you love. Your soul time may not produce immediate answers—then again, it might. It's not a time to analyze or fix. It's a time of flow, like Lukey on the Yuba.

This is how we learn to live *from love* instead of living *for looks*. We slow down long enough to listen and receive the love that is ours for the taking. We let it seep into the deepest parts of our being. In the past, we were moving so fast, talking such a streak, that the goodness would just run off. Now we allow our soul to be soaked—down to the root—and then we get up from the chair and we go about our day from that soul-soaked place.

Practicing twenty minutes of soul time is about allowing God to chip away at the plaster we've packed around our fleshy, vulnerable soul. It's about returning to what he's already given us. Returning instead of relentlessly forging ahead.

So the challenge for all of us will be creating enough space to practice what we know, and then simply believing God at his Word: that as we come to him, we trade our try for his rest.[2] We trade our tangle for his peace.

Take a deep breath and get quiet. Then quieter still. What is God speaking into that true place inside you?

(Remember, don't fight the river.)

Reflection & Expression

Make an appointment with yourself for twenty minutes of soul time. Create space for your soul to speak up, and then ask your soul what it might want to say to you. Once you have written for a bit of time, ask God what he wants to say to you about anything you've written. Remember to keep your pen moving.

Ruthlessly confront anything that threatens this appointment:

Shoulds

Pleasing

Comparison

Perfection

What others think

Productivity

Efficiency

Failure

Doubt

Putting everyone else's needs before your own

For Your Brazen Board

Add a few words—or images representing these words—from your writing, key words that resonate deeply with you. You could also add the words "soul time" and/or images that remind you of a safe place for your soul to speak up.

You could find an image of a river as a reminder to honor the flow in your twenty minutes of soul time instead of evaluating (read "judging") what's emerging.

Or you could find an image that represents grace to you, God coming near to you because he loves you, not because you've earned his presence.

4

Wade Out into Gold

Don't edit your soul according to the fashion.

—Franz Kafka

I drove to the naval base on Coronado, a little island here in San Diego, and grabbed a fish taco to go. Then I had my soul time and my writing time right there on the beach.

It's become clear as I've been emerging from the Hard season that I need to be outside more. When you're in the belly of the whale, you don't think to surface for fresh air. You're just in the darkness, and you have to remind yourself to find the light. But now I'm feeling drawn to the outside, the fresh air, the spaciousness and brightness.

So I follow my intuition to go to the beach.

I spread out my beach blanket, a Moroccan-inspired blue and white throw I love. As I settled in to eat my lunch, I noticed to my right a young woman doing yoga in the world's most microscopic bikini.

Every guy who ran by on the beach just about fell down. The lifeguard circled in his red jeep more times than I believe was actually necessary. I mean, there was no one even in the water near us.

At first it was just sun salutations, but then I look over—as I'm shoving down my fish taco—and she's got one of her legs up in the air. In the world's most microscopic bikini, in case I hadn't mentioned that. And I was like, *Good grief. There are CHILDREN nearby. FAMILIES. DOGS. I'm EATING over here. Put your LEG down.*

Of course I said these things only to myself . . . mostly.

Then a little voice inside me said, "Isn't it interesting that you came to the beach today and there's a woman doing yoga on the beach right here, right where you're sitting? Don't you find that interesting? And isn't it interesting that you're annoyed? Don't you find that interesting?"

Shut up.

I did not find any of it interesting.

And then I remembered an experience I hadn't thought about in years: A long time ago I was talking to a middle-aged woman who was bookish and wore sensible shoes and she told me she danced on the beach as her way of experiencing God.

When she told me this, I was struck dumb. I stood there looking at her with my mouth open, thinking, *I'm sorry, what did you say?* I was so envious of her freedom. To be Plain Jane and to dance and dance and dance. Right there on the beach.

To me, dancing is the embodiment of freedom. I'm a self-conscious dancer. I don't even really wish I were a better dancer. I just wish I were a freer dancer. And the bookish woman, dancing her prayers to God, was FREE.

This hot little Yoga Babe in her itsy-bitsy-teeny-weeny was free too. Oh, yes she was. Maybe she liked the attention. Maybe she needed the attention. I don't know. But the fact that she was comfortable enough to practice yoga right there on the beach . . . well, perhaps, deep down, I was feeling that familiar envy. The envy I felt for Plain Jane.

And then, as I watched Yoga Babe, that little voice inside me said, "You want to edit her in all the ways you edit yourself. You're bothered by her because you perceive her to have something you want: Freedom to be yourself. Freedom to express. Freedom to move." I tried to drown that little voice with my Diet Coke (which I am officially off of except . . . sometimes), but that little voice is surprisingly resilient.

I thought about a recent weekend trip I had taken with My Group to Laguna Beach. Earlier in the night we had gone around the circle and each shared one word we were bringing into the weekend. My word was *saved* because I always feel rescued in their presence. Later, on the balcony at the house we borrowed from Tina's brother, I danced wildly in front of them like I've never danced before. I was startlingly awkward, and it felt good to take up space in the world.

Back at the beach I got up off my blanket and walked right past Yoga Babe and—while dodging men who were practically jogging in place to watch her—stepped into the ocean, which was ice cold and immediately refreshing. I did my 4–7–8 breathing that Erica taught me (inhale for 4 counts, hold for 7 counts, exhale for 8 counts), and I looked down.

The water was so shallow that it was perfectly clear and I could see gold in the sand I was standing on. Like someone had dumped glitter everywhere. It's mica. Flecks of heaven.

I let the water splash up my leggings. Farther than I intended, but it was so hot outside, and it felt good. The coldness felt like it was literally draining the inflammation from my feet, which looked like sausages under the water.

I turned to walk back to my blanket and Yoga Babe's mat was there but she was gone, perhaps cooling off in the water.

And the little voice inside my soul said, "Expand. Expand instead of edit. Expand, Leeana."

(Which, of course, is gold.)

Reflection & Expression

I've edited myself by refusing to _____ .

For Your Brazen Board

Add something gold.

5

Unhook from Heavy

> I sensed that God did not judge my strong urge to fly.
> —Barbara Brown Taylor

I mentioned to you that I'm writing this book at age thirty-nine, on the threshold of turning forty. As it turns out, forty is kind of a giant deal throughout the Hebrew Scripture, used to separate two distinct epochs or eras. I wonder if this is somehow prophetic in my own life. That, in fact, I'm on a threshold of sorts, a new beginning.

If you look in both the Old and New Testaments, you see forty *everywhere*, especially as it relates to God fulfilling a promise to his people (don't forget that part).

Here are just a few highlights: the rains fell on Noah and his family for 40 days and 40 nights; Israel ate manna for 40 years; Moses was with God on the mountain for 40 days and 40 nights; the Israelites roamed the desert for 40 years; Goliath egged on

Israel for 40 days; David reigned for 40 years; Solomon reigned for 40 years; Jesus fasted and was tempted for 40 days; Jesus remained on earth 40 days after his resurrection.

I have a lot of feelings about turning forty. (Actually, I have a lot of feelings about everything.) Some days I feel clammy and gaggy about the whole thing. And then other days I feel this might just be my golden era, the time when I settle in to my skin in a way I have not done previously. And that feels thrilling.

Life did not move at all, crept entirely, through some of my thirties. When our babies were small and the days felt like a complete run-on sentence, lacking any punctuation, the weeks walked on by but the hours crawled. And I could not find a single shred of truth in the eyes of the woman at the grocery store who looked at me longingly and said, "Enjoy every minute. It all goes so fast."

It did not.

Now, with my twins in first grade and the baby in preschool, time is picking up speed, clipping even. And I begin to feel this creeping suspicion that time is not infinite, not in this body anyway. The Soul Bullies tell me my best years are behind me now, and if I didn't enjoy every minute of them—suck the marrow from every second—then I missed out. The bullies hook into my anxiety by telling me I will wake up tomorrow and be eighty and I will feel bereft because I did not prop my eyelids open with toothpicks; I did not take life in nearly enough.

The Soul Bullies are such killjoys, such hope slayers. They add an inordinate weight to our days, huge pressure, making the stakes feel so high all the time. If you aren't happy, then you're miserable. If you aren't celebrating, then you're ungrateful. If you aren't hyper-present, then you're missing it all. And the truth is, life is so much more nuanced than that, isn't it. Some days I need to celebrate into the night. Some days just need to end. God has even given me the capacity to hold space for hope and disappointment in the very same square inch of my soul. But the Soul Bullies are out to eradicate this kind of mystery.

The antidote to the weight is a blessing from the Psalms I've been reciting on repeat lately. It goes like this: "Let the loveliness of our Lord, our God, rest on us, affirming the work that we do. Oh yes. Confirm the work that we do."[1]

This may sound so unexamined, so shallow, but my greatest hope for my forties is lightness. The kind of lightness that comes from the Source. Not a lightness from denial or head-in-the-sand living. Quite the opposite. A lightness that is grace, gift, fruit, harvest that comes from sowing seeds of prayer, silence, stillness, rest.

At St. Gregory's the Great Catholic Church of San Diego, a fountain flows from a cross at a high point on the property down to the entrance, six distinct step-downs of moving water, flowing down the hill. The water coming toward you from the cross symbolizes Christ coming to you, that you do not have to strive after him. He is always moving toward us; we do not have to rely on our attempts or efforts. This is what I want, as I stand on this side of a major life threshold. I want to experience more deeply and fully what Christ has already given me:

"I'm leaving you well and whole. That's my parting gift to you. *Peace.* I don't leave you the way you're used to being left—feeling abandoned, bereft. So don't be upset. Don't be distraught."[2]

In my ongoing twenty minutes of soul time, I begin asking God to heal me of my striving, my proving, my searching for significance, the white-knuckled try that is never enough, never enough. I don't want to continue buying into the lies, grabbing, consuming, hiding. I want another path, a different trajectory, because I know the shame-based striver in me will *never* be satisfied.

God said to me, "I am making you a Brazen Promise. If you will return to me with your heavy, I will give you my light. Put your Striving Self on the couch. Welcome the Striving Leeana. She's tired. She needs compassion and care. Give her a soft place to land. Cover her in the faux fur throw and bring her coffee in the pink Amore mug and some ice water, too, in the hobnail glass. Rub her arm and tell her, 'It's OK. You can rest now. You don't have to try anymore. You're off the clock.' Welcome her with love and acceptance and grace. But whatever you do, Leeana, do not let her get up from the couch. She doesn't get to be in charge anymore."

I am practically desperate at times to secure solutions for myself. Especially when I feel the mind plagues coming for me. My desire for expression and my salvation become interlinked so inextricably that I cannot discern my next step. As gently as is possible, God reminds me to return. He reminds me that nothing, apart from him, is a solution. Nothing. Even the good thing. Even the best thing. Nothing is a solution except him.

If the solution has been provided, then what are we to make of these other pursuits and passions: work, art, marriage, motherhood, community? What are these, then, if they are no solution whatsoever? These pursuits, these passions, are our garden—the place where we have been given exceptional freedom, dominion. The only thing God warned us about was the forbidden, the false solution.

It's excessively painful when we are revealed. When our hiding is revealed. I don't think many of us hide on purpose. I don't think we realize we're doing it at all. We're broken, we're searching, we're tired, and so in our hiding we also grab. We grab at highly destructive things, and we grab at socially acceptable things, and we grab at superspiritual things, all of which result in the same thing: shame. Because we're grabbing at everything else, but we're not returning to God. This grabbing gets weighty.

When we're familiar with lugging our life around—à la living as a Soul Sherpa—it's hard to trust in a lighter way. It's hard to trust God's promises to us that things might be able to change if we do the disciplines of listening and letting go, which is why it's truly tender that God has begun this dialogue with me on the threshold of my fortieth birthday. Perhaps this is his gracious way of affirming the work he is leading me into, a promise that is to come.

As I have put the striving Leeana on the couch, God has reminded me over and over again that as I bring him my heavy, he will return to me his light. The burden will lift incrementally as I continue coming home. Effort will be met with ease. For me, this has meant that all my energy isn't going toward dragging around shame and fear. Instead, my energy is reserved for much more productive matters. Like eating artichokes and giggling with friends.

The minute life starts to feel heavy and breathless again, I stop and ask God, "What do you want to say to me today?" We talk for a bit—usually about unhooking from whatever lie I am buying hook, line, and sinker that day—and my energy level returns. And then, a few days pass, and I have to begin again because I forget.

Jesus already told us about this energy exchange in the Gospel of John, where he says, "I am the vine and you are the branches. Abide in me" (John 15:5, paraphrase mine). Live in me. Make your home in me just as I have made my home in you. Separated, you cannot produce a thing.[3]

The word *abide* literally means "onward wait." Absolute poetry. Abiding is an active stillness. It's unhooking from the strain of striving for significance and, instead, returning to the garden where our significance and our Source are waiting for us.

We don't work or will our way back to the garden. We return to God, hands open wide, and we let him fill them. We hide *in* him, not *from* him.⁴ And the promises—of rescue, of rest, of production, of crop, of shelter, of hope, of wisdom, of forgiveness, of company, of truth—are realized.

Last weekend we went out to Julian, a mountain town about an hour or so outside of San Diego. We walked through grass up to our hips, wind sweeping down the meadow we were tromping through. In one direction you could see cows grazing at the horizon. In the other direction you could see rolling hills covered in trees. The landscape in between was dotted here and there with farmhouses and old barns, a unique scene for us city dwellers. The kids were at least a hundred feet away from me, and the only noises I could hear were their faint laughs and the rustle of the grass in the breeze. A rickety fence was propped up by lichened rocks. Gray greens, sea foam greens, against granite boulders. Wispy white clouds moved overhead like breath. I could see the color. I could hear the world. I could feel life. I was there, in that moment, inside my own body. For that minute or two the loveliness rested on me, like gossamer. I promise you when I tell you that this is a certifiable death-to-life miracle.

Reflection & Expression

Write about an area of your life where you need to "onward wait."

For Your Brazen Board

Add an image of lightness.

Add an image of unhooking.

6

Keep Casting Your Nets

It was my letting go that gave me a better hold.

—Chris Matakas

I have the words "keep casting your nets" written on a kraft envelope and taped to the wall above my desk.

This simple sentence, from a story in the book of John, is offering me some calibration these days. It's a reminder that my response, much more than my results, is what creates meaning in my life. To the point that sometimes I feel like God is saying to me, "Frankly, Leeana, the results are none of your business."

According to the account in Scripture, the disciples were out on the Sea of Galilee fishing. They had spent the entire night casting their nets but caught nothing. Not. One. Thing.

It's dawn. They're exhausted. Their labors seem futile. And someone calls to them from the shore. It's Jesus, though they don't know that immediately. He says, "Cast your nets again on the right side of the boat."

They do, and their nets are so full they can't haul in the catch.

keep = continue showing up bravely and

casting = offering

your = no one else's

nets = what God has put in your hands

Leeana, keep . . .

I cast laundry into the washing machine and then into the dryer. I cast dishes into warm, soapy water. I cast tubes of yogurt into lunch bags and meals into the oven. I cast words into the world. I cast love out to my children, my husband, my family, my friends. Some days, this feels mostly effortless, like I'm smack-dab in the center of what I was made to do and be. And then there are the other days. When I'm filled with self-doubt because nothing seems to be working.

And God says, "Keep doing the work I have given you today. Continue the work of feeding, nurturing, creating, ideating, hoping, holding, wondering, believing, listening. Keep doing the sacred work. Do not grow weary in doing good because at the right time, the fullness will materialize."[1]

Trusting our try over the mystery of God's miracles is not freedom; it's fear. Paralysis and cynicism are ways we distrust him and doubt ourselves. He's asking us to show up, come out from behind our fear of failure or fear of purposelessness. We have the choice whether or not we will do the vulnerable work of showing up. Participation, not perfection, is what's so brazen.

Leeana, keep casting . . .

Every day, God asks me to cast the nets of mothering, marriage, and making. Some days I'm sure I don't have what it takes to offer what God is asking me to offer. These words taped to my wall serve as a reminder to keep showing up even on the days when I'm plagued with self-doubt, even on the days when I'm a stammering Moses. Even on those days, which are most days, when I am to keep giving my offering.

What's interesting is that the etymology of the word *offering* implies a sacrificial element. So it follows that our offering is not something we come by easily. It's something we fight for. It's something that costs us. I will not offer that which costs me nothing.[2] An offering is something we give away. It's something we let go of. It's something we set down. You can't really offer something and keep your hands on it. You're giving this love, this creation, this artistry, this contribution, this dream . . . away.

I heard a podcast with Oprah Winfrey in which she was talking about the origins of her epic documentary series on faith, "Belief." She related a conversation she and Maya Angelou had years ago when Angelou made this prophetic comment: "Oprah, right now you're in show business. But someday you're going to be about your Father's business."

Oprah said she spent her entire adult life listening to other people, and now *she* had something to say. Her message to the world, and her fulfillment of Maya Angelou's prediction, is this documentary. Oprah personally financed the entire enterprise because, she said, and these were exact words, "It is my offering." Isn't that beautiful.

Doesn't it make sense that real, enduring purpose comes from sacrificially giving back to God what he has put into our hands and trusting that what is meant to come back to us will, in fact, come back to us?

For any number of reasons, some of you have given up on what you want to offer, and God is still standing on the shore, asking you to cast your nets one more time. Perhaps you've ditched your desires because your nets have come up empty one too many times. Maybe it has nothing to do with how many fish you are or aren't going to catch on this cast. Maybe, instead, it has everything to do with the vulnerability of offering your soul even with no guarantees.

Because here's what strikes me: Nothing in the fishing story changed from the late-night net casting to the early-dawn net casting. The lake was still the same. The fish were still the same. The boat was still the same. I'd even bet the guys' casting technique was still the same. The disciples had done nothing different.

So what changed? God called. They responded. That's the only thing we know of that changed. The call and response turned emptiness to fullness. While I very much like the happy ending of this story, I wonder if the disciples' *response*, more than the *results*, is the point of the narrative.

If we respond to God's call, will he change our luck? I'm not so sure. I do know, however, that he'll touch our hearts. We want to catch a solution in our nets. He wants to be our Savior, to be the voice we listen to. And there is something about continuing to cast even when, especially when, we are not in control that changes us.

We fold another load of laundry. We pack a lunch. We tend to an elderly parent. We show up at the soup kitchen. We kick butt at a board meeting. We create space to listen. We take the time to create. We get our hands moving. We do the work.

Leeana, keep casting your . . .

If you don't know what *you* are supposed to be offering, if you have no idea at all, it's OK. I'm here to tell you, it's OK. There's a soul-spinning amount of talk about calling and vocation. So much so that a girl could wind up feeling like she's the only one in the world who doesn't know exactly what she's supposed to be investing her time and energy in.

I don't think we can ever go wrong with asking God to help us see what we are to offer. I truly believe he wants to show us because I know that one of the saddest things in all the world is when we believe we've got to be something other or different from God's design.

You are just to keep casting *your* nets. We do not compare our nets to someone else's, our cast to someone else's, our haul to someone else's. It's practically impossible to keep our wandering eyes off everyone else's work and focus on the task we have been given for the day. But I believe, as you undoubtedly do, that comparison is one of the biggest traps there is.

Friend, just do you. And if you don't know what it means to "do you," then start there in your next twenty minutes of soul time.

Leeana, keep casting your nets . . .

I look down at my hands to see what God has put in them and I return to that work, that love, that doing, that dabbling. Daily, I ask God to help me focus less and less on *results* and more and more on my *response*.

I cast my nets again. I fold another load of laundry for my family: Steve's uniform, Luke's baseball jersey, the girls' *Frozen* pajamas. I hold a child close to me. I turn toward my husband. I pick up a pen.

Some days I have trouble reconciling the demands of what's been placed in my hands with my own resources. Such was the case with practically every human in the Bible: "You want me to do what, God? You want me to go where? You want me to say what? To whom? Uh, I think you've got the wrong guy."

We cast the love nets over our kids, but we have no control over whether or not they will "turn out." We cast nets over our work, but we cannot strangle our work into submission or success. That doesn't mean we give up. It just means we learn to give up the white-knuckling that comes from thinking it's all up to us. Our codependence on our work, on our kids, on our results is not where we flourish. If anything, that death-grasp is where we wither.

Instead, we ask God to show us how we might cast our nets from our "onward wait"—our abiding—instead of our effort. We ask God to show us how to hold the tension of our response and the results. We ask God to remind us, yet again, that it's all holy. The laundry, the making, the moving, the shaking, the dabbling, the desiring, the dreaming, the waking. It's all holy. The rest is none of our business.

Reflection & Expression

God, in what area of my life are you asking me to keep casting my nets?

For Your Brazen Board

What are some of the offerings you cast out into the world? Find an image that represents that offering.

Add the words "keep casting your nets" or "it's all holy" or "the results are none of my business."

7

See the Pepper Tree

He knows your weakness. He wants only your love, wants only the chance to love you.

—Mother Teresa of Calcutta

I was having coffee with a friend the other day. She was telling me how her life isn't arriving in the time or packaging she assumed it would, and she admitted something to me I haven't been able to get out of my mind since she said it.

She said, *"I feel like I'm behind."*

If we're honest, most of us have to admit we feel at least a step behind in the day to day of life. Behind on starting dinner. Behind on school permission slips. Behind on gym visits. Behind on laundry. Behind on email. Behind on work deadlines. Behind on sleep. We wake up, and we're already behind.

So there's the right-under-the-surface frenzy of feeling like life is always one step ahead, and we are always lagging or lacking in some way. But then there's also the deeper, and perhaps even more toxic, brand of "behind."

I'm behind on life. I'm behind on getting married. I'm behind on starting a family. I'm behind on having a second child. I'm behind on my career. I'm behind on getting thin. I'm behind on the trends. I'm behind on buying a house. Life milestones are supposed to be arriving—they're arriving for everyone else—but I can't keep up with where I'm supposed to be, where I thought I'd be.

If we've decided to stay home with our kids, then we feel behind on our career. If we've decided to pursue our career, then we feel behind on starting a family. If we've prioritized our education, then we feel behind on getting married. If we've married young, then we feel behind on the personal enrichment others have had the time and space to pursue.

My friend put her finger on something I believe so many of us, no matter what our age or stage, are up against: for any number of reasons within or beyond our control *we feel behind.* I wonder how many of us are living out of that internal pressure to catch up and keep up . . . maybe even more than we realize.

What happens when we ask our desires to arrive in certain ways, unfortunately, is that we end up squeezing the neck of life. We end up grasping for control, which you may have guessed by now is not living from your soul. It's living from your striving.

Steve's job in the Navy has required us to move around a bit. Because of this nomadic lifestyle, I have been practically desperate at times for a home. Not just a house, but a homestead, roots, the sense that we are spreading out and settling in for the long haul.

I want a home where my grandchildren will visit someday. I want a home with height marks on the wall and little handprints in the cement. I want a home where I have put my touch in every room, have had the time and opportunity to make it my own.

But we don't have that kind of life. Not yet, anyway.

Some of my friends do. One in particular has a gorgeous ranch-style home with stonework and beams and two fireplaces and a guesthouse. I envy her stability, and when I look at her life, those gnarly Soul Bullies whisper, *You're behind on creating this kind of life for your kids. They're missing out on memories because you don't have this.*

The more my other friends have this sense of long-term stability, the more I try to wring it out of *my* life, and the less and less it arrives.

All I do by trying to force the fantasy is make myself and my husband crazy, and I miss what's happening right under my nose in the glorious impermanence of our life today. (Sigh.)

Everything I throw into the need-to-catch-up-and-keep-up— new pillows, Pinterest boards, Pottery Barn catalogs—is consumed. The only way out is to take Christ's hand, the one he is always extending to me, offering me a way back to him.

The problem is, Christ so very rarely offers us the solution we believed would make everything feel better. Usually the answer isn't finding a husband or the perfect house or the next child or the promotion to partner. Usually the relief from all this hot pursuit arrives because we finally stand still long enough to let ourselves be loved.

We get our heads out of the sky and/or the sand, and put one foot in front of the other—right here in this asking-for-our-presence life. Life doesn't demand our presence. It asks. And we decide whether or not we will tolerate the beauty we're currently standing on.

The temptation, I believe, is to become convinced that our life is out there somewhere and we must go out and take hold of it . . . when, in fact, our life is right here waiting for us to notice it.

We all want something that isn't arriving in the timing we'd assumed it would. And that's OK. These are desires of our heart. They are soul-longings. They are good things. We absolutely must allow ourselves to hold space for these dreams. They deserve to be honored and recognized, not shoved down while we tell ourselves we'd be happy if we'd just be more grateful or more content.

The problem isn't desire. The problem is what we do with our desire when we feel like we're behind in satisfying it.

Another friend of mine was going through a particularly unsettling season of life. Her husband had been continually underemployed, they had amassed a staggering amount of debt, and she was raising a slew of children while her husband was trying to work extra hours.

She was afraid. Afraid of losing everything. Life felt like it was teetering on the edge, even after they had worked hard and tried to make responsible decisions with their work and home and family.

A wise mentor told her, "God didn't promise you a certain lifestyle. In fact, God didn't promise you a home. God didn't promise that you wouldn't be homeless. God didn't even promise you minimum wage. God promised you his love. You might be homeless. You might need to get a job cleaning toilets. But that doesn't mean he doesn't love you."

If this isn't a donkey kick to the stomach, I don't know what is.

We all know God didn't promise us our dream spouse or dream home or dream family or dream job. We *know* that. And yet, when those things don't arrive or when they are threatened, it's easy to panic.

Someone said to me recently, "I'm beginning to realize I want security more than I want a Savior."

Whoa.

I could write so much here about how waiting strengthens us and how it forces us to rely on God and trust his perfect timing.

But I'm not sure how helpful hearing about all that actually is. The fact is, it's practically intolerable when life arrives book rate, especially after we had paid extra for Amazon Prime.

Why do some people get their dream home, their dream mate, their dream family, their dream job, their dream financial situation, their dream car, their dream guest cottage, their dream vacation, and others don't? Well, I can think of a thousand reasons, and then also a thousand rebuttals to those reasons. All of which is to say, I don't know. So perhaps I am asking the wrong question.

Maybe the right question is this: Whether I'm overwhelmingly behind or impressively ahead, do I believe God loves me? Do I believe I'm loved no matter what arrives and no matter when it arrives?

(I know. Such overly aggressive questions.)

Kathleen Norris writes, "For grace to be grace, it must give us things we didn't know we needed and take us places where we didn't know we didn't want to go. As we stumble through the crazily altered landscape of our lives, we find that God is enjoying our attention as never before."[1]

When the landscape of our lives is "crazily altered," frankly, it sucks. I don't love dealing with the fact that things are not what I thought they'd be. We find the landscape to be unfamiliar, unforgiving, or just plain empty.

I want to be very good at acceptance. I'm not. I can get so wild-eyed about my brilliant ideas and making sure they get accomplished. The more I take my meds and breathe, the more I see how very brazen it is to stop pushing and be still, to come to God with both our hands open.

We hold our current reality in one hand and hold our longings in the other hand, and we ask God to show us how we can honor both.

This is the holiest of work because it requires us to let go of our compulsion to secure our own solutions.

I don't think God is asking us to suppress or "get over" our dreams. And I don't think he wants us to miss out on the sacred ground we're standing on either.

There's a small, empty plot of land at the bottom of our property. I always look at it longingly because, in my mind, it's the absolute perfect spot for a little guesthouse. It's currently overgrown by a listing pepper tree that creates a canopy under which Luke likes to hide out and whittle. Yes, whittle.

He invited me to crawl into the canopy the other day. I got down on my hands and knees and inched my way through the branches and leaves. When I got inside, he said, "Look, Mom, you can stand up." And much to my surprise, he was right. The tree had grown in such a way that once I passed through the branches that touched the ground, I was inside a chamber of green, the light seeping in through the hundreds of thousands of portals in the leaves. And I could stand up all the way.

"Isn't it so cool, Mom?" Luke said.

"Yeah, baby," I said. "It's so cool."

Reflection & Expression

Are you feeling behind in any area of your life?

For Your Brazen Board

Find an image of something you desire.

Write or collage the word: "Loved."

8

Look through the Divine View-Master

Beauty is the mystery hidden in each of us waiting to be found.

—Adrienne Sandvos

If we're willing, I think God will divulge to us—one by one—the places and spaces where we are captive. If we want to know. If we want to be free.

Of course, if we open ourselves up to learning more about these spaces and places, if we decide to turn toward our own captivity and hiding, we're likely welcoming a giant ordeal. You know, a real ruckus. Sometimes it's easier just to look the other way. And yet, tiptoeing around them is, I'm finding, worse. Sometimes Brazen Work means bobbing for time bombs.

Our friend Ken asked me with a hint of skepticism, "Leeana, are you a shoe girl?"

I hesitated and then bobbled the answer because it was so completely clear and unclear to me at the same time.

You know those moments when someone puts their finger on something you've been trying to avoid and pretend about. And you think you've done a pretty good job keeping your own smoke and mirrors going and then someone, unknowingly, outs you.

Throughout my dating career—which was spotty and strained—I managed to look primarily for men who were as close to six foot five as I could find them. I was always drawn to hulking guys. I can say, confidently, that being with supersized men made me feel (1) taken care of and (2) small. Two things I believed men could offer me.

When you're a woman with big hands and big feet and broad shoulders and, let's just say, an "athletic build," it feels good to feel miniature next to someone else. It feels good to feel both childlike and also petite. It feels good to be physically reduced.

And then Steve and I met, and in a whirlwind, we were engaged. He was not—physically anyway—the kind of guy I usually picked. He is exactly one inch taller than me. He is certainly very muscular and fit but not hulking, per se. I am not significantly smaller than he is. In fact, to the naked eye, there is probably no perceivable height difference between us. And if I wear shoes with any kind of heel and he wears his annoyingly paper-thin flip-flops, then—you guessed it—I am taller.

In the beginning, I looked past all this. I was interested in his intensity and wooed by his unwavering pursuit of me. I put aside my "type" and listened to the voices that said sometimes God brings you what you least expect, in the packages you least expect them, which is true.

Right after we were married, we moved overseas for Steve's job, and as we were in the final stages of packing, I lined up all my shoes and decided—perhaps subconsciously—to give away the pairs with the highest heels.

I gave my sister some red wedges that I loved.

For the longest time I was a shoe horse. In fact, on volleyball trips in high school and college, I would always take two bags: one with clothes, one with shoes. So it surprised me—stopped me, actually—when Ken asked me if I was a "shoe girl."

"Of course I'm a shoe girl, Ken. How is that not completely obvious?"

But I realized I had stopped being a shoe girl since Steve and I got married. Shoes have represented a major dilemma for me. I stopped buying shoes I loved because I didn't want to risk appearing taller than Steve. I stopped wearing shoes I loved because I let my self-consciousness around our height difference override my own taste.

I have badgered myself by thinking things like, *A more mature woman wouldn't care, wouldn't notice, wouldn't think about something so trivial. A more secure woman would flaunt her height with six-inch heels. A more self-possessed woman wouldn't go to such trouble to try to be so small.*

And maybe all that's true. But here I am: insecure, caring, noticing.

I watched a TED Talk by Amy Cuddy about the science behind our nonverbal communication, specifically the power dynamics associated with our posture. Her research shows that when we try to make ourselves smaller physically—by hunching, collapsing in on ourselves, crossing our arms in front of us, crossing our legs—our desire to be more diminutive literally affects our hormonal composition, making us feel less powerful. Conversely, when we open up our bodies and occupy more space with our arms and legs, this shift in posture also affects our hormones—specifically an increase in testosterone (dominance hormone) and a decrease in cortisol (stress hormone). When we expand our bodies for two minutes, we literally feel more powerful and less stressed.

Crazy, right?

Cuddy's research also includes nonverbal communication as it relates to gender, and—you guessed it—women tend to chronically feel less powerful than men and therefore try to make their bodies appear smaller more often than men do.

For those of you who have spent any amount of time trying to be small in life—silent, apologetic, shamed, opinionless, miniature—you get how a girl could go through her whole life wearing flats while all she can think about are those red wedges.

When Ken asked me about the shoes, I had to confront what I thought I was managing just fine. The truth is, I've given up parts of myself to feed an anxiety. Deeper still, I'm not experiencing a sense of spaciousness around my own body. Not completely. And, frankly, I want to spend time thinking about other things. I want to spend my precious minutes thinking about something other than how I can look smaller in relation to Steve.

God whispers to me, "Don't put your best energy toward contempt, self-consciousness. Don't spend your time feeding the Soul Bullies. Put your best energy toward loving and holding and creating and dancing and laughing."

Always calling us to deeper freedom.

I would like to feel a greater sense of comfort in my own skin, and not as it is defined in relation to someone else's skin but because I have done the harrowing work of making peace with my personhood. If I'm looking to Steve's height as the source of my own sense of beauty, then I'm sunk. Steve will never be tall enough to heal me. I will never find flat-enough flats to heal me. *The work must be done from the inside out.*

If it's true that love drives out fear, then I want nothing short of radical acceptance, radical love. For my body and for Steve's body. When shame is my lens, my eyes are unreliable. I need the Divine View-Master—so I can see myself as I was meant to be seen.

When we're living out of shame, perceived shortcomings are our absolute demise. We have to protect ourselves from giving the world any evidence that we are not good enough.

When we're living from our Created Center, we don't have to worry if someone sees a chink in our armor. We don't have to be so self-protected. We don't have to blameshift. We don't have to lie. We don't have to spend our entire life in flats if we don't truly want to. We can stand in the nakedness of our humanity and not be ashamed. We can tell the truth because we have come to believe that nothing about our externals determines our worth.

This is really hard, though, right?

Sometimes I wonder if God's saying, "Yeah, I got it, you're not perfect. But do you know you are beautiful?" Do you? Do I? Do we believe we are actually, in our own mysterious ways, beautiful?

I heard Glennon Melton speak recently on the topic of being beautiful. Here's her theory: Beautiful means being full of beauty. Every time you observe beauty, you are filling yourself up with more and more and more beauty. Someone who is beautiful, then, is someone who fills up on beauty in this world whenever and wherever she finds it—enjoying the sea, reading to her kids, holding hands on a hike, laughing till she cries, ingesting poetry like it's protein.

Many of us have internalized the idea that being beautiful means taking up the smallest amount of space possible. Mary Pipher talks about the danger of this notion in her book *Reviving Ophelia*. She believes part of anorexia, in her estimation, is a message to the world that says, "I will take up only a small amount of space. I won't get in the way."[1]

Whenever I wrestle with my own qualms about my body, I am immediately reminded of the four female eyes staring up at me in my home. Will I teach these girls how to take up their God-appointed space in this world? With dignity. With beauty. With self-possession. They will watch me to know how to do this. They will watch me play small. Or they will watch me occupy space. They will determine how to feel about their bodies by listening to me talk about mine, watching me hide mine.

This is no joke.

I watch the two of them and learn from them too. During a recent misty rain, three-year-old Elle runs into the house while I'm putting away groceries. The next thing I know she is standing in the courtyard outside our front door, wearing not one stitch, arms stretched out above her, in a rain-induced trance. Naked and unashamed. Glimpses of the garden lost.

Sometimes I practice being taller than Steve. He'll wear those deeply problematic flip-flops to church and I'll deliberately put on a four-inch wedge. I stand next to him, singing, feeling uncomfortable. Like a gigantor-girl—Goliath.

The only thing I know to do is to keep welcoming the discomfort instead of avoiding it. I just keep practicing the holy prayer practice of "Height Therapy." Or maybe, more accurately, "Space Therapy." I keep learning how to take up space in this world, unapologetically. If not for me, then for my girls.

Reflection & Expression

Find an image that defines beauty for you—try looking for something that is a nontraditional representation of beauty. In other words, don't just look for the most perfect model in a magazine.

Write about why you chose that particular image.

For Your Brazen Board

Add your beauty-image.

9

Seek and Find

There is only one problem on which all my existence, my peace, and my happiness depend: to discover myself in discovering God. If I find Him I will find myself and if I find my true self I will find Him.

—Thomas Merton

In my attempts to spend more time with my soul, I am simultaneously spending more time with God. I see how our self-discovery is inextricably linked to our God-discovery and vice versa.

Our perceptions of ourselves are not the only falsities keeping us in hiding. Our notions of God are every bit as responsible for compelling us to cower instead of join him in the cool of the morning.

I know this is true of me, especially when I have quieted my life and my soul and I am making the space to listen. Often, then, I realize I don't know exactly who I'm talking to, who I'm waiting for, who I'm looking for.

In *Wearing God*, Lauren Winner affirms my sense of ambiguity with the reminder that the "Bible invites us to imagine God: in some very singular ways; in dizzingly hundreds of ways; sometimes, in no way at all."[1] If this is true of Scripture, and I believe it is, then how are we to think of God when we are on our back patios, scribbling down our deepest longings? How are we to think about God in the quiet spaces where we meet? How are we to picture God's face, if in fact a face is even helpful?

I did not grow up with a man in my house, but I did grow up with the primary image of God as a middle-aged male. When I think about God that way, sitting in my living room wanting to get to know me, it feels kind of creepy, frankly. At the very least, this image does not compel me to intimacy or connection. If anything, I'm uncomfortable. I don't believe God's primary desire is to see how comfortable he can make us, but I do believe God visited people throughout the Scriptures in many forms and faces. And so, could I allow my image of God to expand beyond middle-aged male? And, in fact, might God be inviting me to do so?

God knows our stories. He knows I'm guarded when it comes to men. He wants us to be able to see him, sit with him, listen. So he arrives in a burning bush or a cloud or a pillar of fire. He arrives as a dove or a warrior or a child. He arrives as a teacher, a carpenter, a preacher. He arrives as a healer, a friend, a mother. He arrives as a son, a Savior, a strong wind. He arrives incarnate—in the ways we can see, touch, taste, and experience him.

To that end, I asked God to expand my view of his face and his presence. I asked God to help me know him more deeply and fully, to help me let go of the barriers between us. One of the greatest gifts of this prayer is God's reminder to me that the Triune God transcends gender.

"What language can I borrow?" says an old hymn. And it's true. Language is so restrictive when it comes to talking about God, especially in the realm of gender. Throughout this book I use male pronouns for God, and—honestly—I do that, especially in this chapter, haltingly, reluctantly. I don't want to alarm anyone or create barriers for anyone by calling God something that feels like I'm taking far too much license, and causes us all to wonder if we're talking about the same Person. And yet I find language, the English language anyway, so limiting in this instance.

Which is why, perhaps, God has given us a rich imagination and the gift of so many different forms and faces of him in the Bible. Our task, in my estimation, is to believe this permission-giving God has offered us far more freedom to engage with him than we realize and that he waits for us to come to him so he can show us his love and compassion.[2]

In his limitless love and compassion, God reminded me of a beautiful image of him: the feminine nature of God . . .

God as someone who creatively engages my senses with beauty. Beauty speaks to me like nothing else. It opens my mind up when life feels small. It comforts me and helps me breathe when my body feels tight. Beauty is my soul language, the way God communicates with my soul. When I lean into the feminine nature of God, I see this wildly creative Spirit that is wooing *my* wildly creative spirit to emerge. I feel seen and heard and known. I feel celebrated. I feel challenged to lean into this soul language more fully. This is the voice and nature of God that nudges me to follow all that is creative in my being.

God as gentle caretaker. When I am running hard and my body is yelling at me and my mind is swirling, this gentle voice of God is the one that reminds me how to treat myself as a companion instead of turn on myself as a critic. This is the voice and nature of God that pats my arm and pours me coffee in my pink Amore mug and sits me down in my pretty Ikat chair by the fireplace. This is the voice and nature of God that help me rest, recover. This is the Comforter.

And, *God as warrior mother.* Defender, protector, armed and battle-ready. This fierce matriarch stands between danger and her daughter, saying, "I created you. Your life needs to be about . . .

returning to

celebrating

living out of

not apologizing for

cultivating

honoring

investigating

standing up for

protecting

championing

loving

the way I created you."

Imagine God leaning toward you and telling you those things. You'd listen. You'd let *your* longings and God's love collide. You'd let your guard down incrementally. You'd come out from hiding.

Can you close your eyes and imagine a place, a space, where all of you and all of God dwell? What does God look like? If you can't picture this exchange, could you ask God to reveal himself to you in a way that brings you safety and comfort?

73

It is a brazen thing to go in search of God, to seek his face, to keep our eyes open for him, to watch for his works, to be alert to the signs of his presence.[3] Inevitably we will have to confront things we don't want to confront. Both about our perceptions of this Being and then, also, about ourselves, especially if we believe we were created in this Being's image.

I once heard someone say God is not behind us, pushing us forward in life. He is, instead, standing out in front of us, already inhabiting the space in front of us, inviting us toward him, his arms reaching out for us as we stumble and fumble in his general direction. Like, "Come on, you can do it, take another step, this way, I'm here, keep going."

Reflection & Expression

What is one barrier that is keeping you from deeper connection and authenticity with God?

God, you are my _____.

For Your Brazen Board

Letting yourself be completely open to what you are drawn to, find an image that reminds you of God.

10

Believe in Beginnings

Still, the profound change
has come upon them: rooted, they
grip down and begin to awaken
—William Carlos Williams,
"Spring and All"

I haven't told anyone this yet, but my first book is now out of print.

It would be hard for me to adequately quantify the amount of my soul that went into that project. How much time and attention and energy. How many tears and fears and hopes. It would be hard for me to take you through the entire winding journey. A journey that started in the Middle East and ended . . . recently . . . these nine years later.

What do you do when your dream goes out of print? When something you created and nourished is now defunct?

You cry. At least a little, I guess.

And then you question the whole entire experience: You begin to believe in the idea that your work is average, or even below average. You begin to believe that results are the only way we measure success anymore. You start second-guessing what you thought you heard rumbling around in your soul all those years ago, what you thought you heard God say straight to your heart.

I've been sitting with these story lines, tugging at them for resolution. I'm wired to want answers to my questions. Why is this the outcome? What was the point of that entire winding road? Why did *that* happen in *that* way?

I'm sure you can relate in your own way. Something you've poured yourself into does not materialize. Something you believed in evaporates. And, if you're honest, you admit you're not quite sure what the entire experience was about. What light is that season shining on today?

My quest for answers got me thinking about the last decade. About God opening a door. About me walking through that door. And then a protracted process of working on my craft. In the midst of that protracted process, I got pregnant with twins, and I—as I'm prone to do—got it all figured out: how I was going to finish the manuscript and turn it in and then give birth to twins and then release the book to modest but meaningful acclaim while holding my two newborns in matching outfits . . . all in that order.

But, wouldn't you know, it didn't go that way. At all.

I worked and I struggled and I shredded and I started over and then I did all those things all over again. Like, roughly, two hundred times. I felt like I was using every bit of precision I had, all in an attempt to hit a moving target.

So there I was, a million months pregnant with my Tiny Tanks, realizing my belly wasn't the only thing growing. What was growing, additionally, was the reality that I was not going to be able to finish the project before the twins came. And I didn't. And they did. And I cried.

Because I had no idea how to do any of the things God had put in my hands. Or so it seemed.

I was able, a few months later, to get the project finished enough and submitted. I was able to rock and cuddle and admire my gorgeous babies even though I felt like the big fish had come up to the surface where I was treading water and had swallowed me whole.

I sat in the belly of the whale and typed and nursed and typed and nursed. Every fourth day I'd shower. And so on. Somehow, this rhythm sustained me, now that I look back. At a time when I was scared and fragile and unsure of who I was as a person, I had the gift of a place to pour out my creative soul.

I guess I can see how God loved me through that specific journey, in that time and space. He threw me a lifeline. And I grabbed it. I, in fact, clutched at it, clenched it, begging him to not let me go into the dark abyss that felt just at my heels.

And he didn't. He hasn't. The days between then and now have not always been easy. There have been seasons since when I've sat in the belly of the whale, wondering where I was and how I got there. I have looked for a window, some light, when there has been very little.

But I've written. And that has been a grace and a kind of therapy.

Today, I can report that I have been gloriously spit up onto the shore of my life and am no longer in the bowels of the great animal. Don't get me wrong, Hard still revisits, still knocks on my door. But now I can begin again. Now I have more fight in me.

I believe God is saying to me that the story is not just about a book being written and launching out into the world and then going out of print. It's not a bait and switch. I didn't get duped by my dreams. This isn't a cruel cosmic joke.

In fact, there's a meta-narrative, a story within a story. And here it is: It's the story of me being unmoored and God tethering me to his dock, saying, "I will not let you lose yourself." It's the story of me with two babies and a deadline. And maybe, just maybe, it all saved me.

"You are loved.

You are loved.

Leeana, you are loved."

Maybe it saved me from the great animal. Maybe it's the work I've been given to help heal me. As St. Gregory the Great said, "There are some so restless that when they are free from labour they labour all the more, because the more leisure they have for thought, the worse interior turmoil they have to bear." Um, yes.

Perhaps this work will always be about settling me and saving me as much as it is about sending work off into the world. I hope that doesn't sound bad, or like I'm not thinking about you.

In fact, I *am* thinking about you. Because I bet there's work God's put in your hands to do, work that perhaps hasn't unfolded in the ways and timing you'd imagined or hoped. Or you're being asked to do it and you don't know exactly how or when or what it's supposed to look like. But here you are, compelled. And somehow that work is, maybe even without you knowing it, keeping your head above water.

Could this be the truest form of vocation: the work that heals us when we do it, somehow, through God's economy, ends up healing others too.

This cannot be a mistake.

Last year, in anticipation of Easter, I kept hearing the following over and over: "What in your life is in need of a resurrection?" Certainly this is the theme of every Easter, but last year for some reason, I kept hearing that same question as it related to my own life, my own journey. Not just as it related to Jesus coming out of the grave, literally, but how that truth is working its way into my own story.

Right before Easter, I got news of this first-book death. And it stung. It stings still. It is incredibly difficult to watch something important to you die: whether that's a relationship, a person, a desire, a dream. You never get used to it. I don't think death ever becomes less abrupt.

But the invitation I kept hearing over and over was to identify an area of my life that needed a resurrection and then BELIEVE that a resurrection could be possible. In other words, hope. Not the noun hope, the verb hope. To hope. Actively.

The ability to hope comes from the idea that *what we believe is the end may be only the beginning.*

Which, of course, is the story of Jesus. For Easter, my pastor spoke on the passage in Luke 24 when Cleopas and his companion are walking on the road to Emmaus and the resurrected Jesus joins them, but they don't know it's him.

The story reads, "Jesus himself came up and walked along with them; but they were kept from recognizing him" (15–16 NIV).

I can think of a few really big things in my life that could use an injection of breath and heartbeat and spirit and vitality. And there's a certain dangerousness to hoping because it puts us out there on a limb of desire that may not produce.

But I don't think the cynics win. I don't think hopelessness wins. And the story from the road to Emmaus makes me wonder if it's at all possible that, in fact, Jesus *himself* is walking in my midst and maybe I'm just not yet recognizing him.

For me, one of the ways Jesus himself is walking with me right now is through the lines of Langston Hughes's poem, "Harlem": "What happens to a dream deferred? Does it dry up . . . *Or does it explode?*"

What happened to Jesus and his followers and their dreams of a new way of living and loving and believing? What happened at the cross? Did it all dry up? Or did it explode?

I'm holding on to the Easter story today as a reminder that sometimes what we believe is an ending might be only the beginning. And, with Jesus, new is always near.

Death stings. Hope explodes.

So here is what I'm putting my hope in today: I'm offering to the world that which God put in my hands to create. And I hope you are too. I hope you make something beautiful today. Not for the critics or the crowds, who will never be perfectly pleased or appeased. But because you have a gift that is pushing its way up through your soul. Your Created Center wants passage through your hands.

We have a whisper-pink lily growing in an otherwise barren dirt patch beside our house. You can see the tops of its onion-y bulb poking up out of the ground and then the single lily shooting skyward. I walk past the bloom when I go down to my studio, and it catches my attention because of something so delicate coming up from something so desolate.

When I look at where that lily comes from, I can't help but believe.

Reflection & Expression

Do you have a dream to do something? What does it look like right now?

How does God intersect with this dream?

What does God have to say to you about this dream?

For Your Brazen Board

Find an image of hope.

11

Allow for Expansion

I want to unfold. Let no place in me hold itself closed for where I am closed, I am false.

—Rainer Maria Rilke, *The Book of Hours*

Our back patio is one of my favorite spaces in our home. You already know I like going there for some soul time now and then. I also like meeting houseguests out there for morning coffee. Steve and I put the kids to bed and head out there with a charcuterie plate and a glass of wine and talk into the night. I like staying up late with friends and family, perched on that patio. The bricks and the wrought iron and the view and the breeze in the palms all seem to work together to get us all talking—first about sports, let's say, then about theology, and then, always, later into the evening, the language shifts to soul talk, which is probably why I love that patio so much.

If you were sitting on my back patio with me at my favorite time of day—dusk—you would see a thousand different skies between twilight and darkness. And you'd see a thousand different views of the trees and the hills and the city below because, as the light changes, the landscape changes. And in that sacred space suspended between the ground below and the sky above, you see that the same thing can look a hundred different ways, all of which will catch your breath.

I've been reading a fascinating book called *Yearnings* by Rabbi Irwin Kula.[1] He says one of our greatest longings as humans is to know exactly who we are, to go on a quest to identify that one elusive True Self we need to be living from.

I have at times in my life been obsessed with this idea. If I can just identify the me I am supposed to be, then I can live freely and wildly as I was made to live. This has proven problematic because as soon as I attempt to define this one, enduring "me," I immediately see that there are many different aspects to me. Like you, I'm not one self. I am a strange amalgamation of different, sometimes seemingly contradictory selves: athlete, creator, nurturer, ideator, homemaker, extrovert, introvert, football fan, poetry lover. I've often erroneously believed I must trade each of these in for the next, instead of learning the fine art of embracing all these different aspects of my identity, letting each of them inform the collective me that is becoming.

I am no longer a college athlete, but today I need to honor aspects of that fierce competitor, that confident leader, that hard worker, that gym rat. I don't just ditch her for the new-and-improved model. She is still with me, wanting to help me with the responsibilities in front of me today.

The temptation for me is to say, "That is no longer me; *this* is now me" and abandon parts of myself as irrelevant or no longer. Kula challenged my thinking about identity when he said we will never be able to identify our one permanent self.

In fact, the Hebrew word for life—*hayim*—is actually plural: *lives*. He suggests, then, that we are a dynamic unfolding of many selves.

Let me give you an example: Steve is a military man, through and through. He joined the Navy because he wanted to serve his country and he still feels compelled to serve. Another side of Steve would love to live on one million acres with a farmhouse and a pond and animals. He would tend this land and he would harvest animals for our food. He'd hang prosciutto and he'd pour wine. He'd line up tables under the trees and he'd invite people to come try wild game or raw cheese. He'd talk into the night about how he hunted and harvested and then prepared every bite. He'd talk about the wines he'd paired and why. He'd tell stories, if anyone wanted to hear. He'd light a fire and invite anyone and everyone to stay as long as they could.

Steve is as much warrior as he is farmer. He is as much father as he is host. I promise you. He speaks French and he shoots guns. He is an executive-level leader and he wants to home-school our kids personally. He makes homemade stock, loves Twain, and fills our house with taxidermy. He's a complicated individual, and doing life next to such a nuanced human being has given me more and more permission to be that way too.

I think we all have something inside us that needs to come out. Maybe it's words. Maybe it's pottery. Maybe it's the most gorgeous meal. Maybe it's a new business model. Maybe it's an herb garden. Maybe it's a marketing strategy. We have things locked or trapped down in the annals of our soul and we need the glorious midwives of this world to help us birth those things that are pressing on us, asking to be released. If Steve pigeon-holed himself into being only one version of himself, he, our family and friends, and the world would miss out on the fascinating fullness that is Steve Tankersley.

I've been through seasons when I felt like I was losing myself. Most of those seasons were defined by my anxious over-responsibility, which led me to believe the free and wild parts of me were gone forever.

If I would have known then what I know now, I would have realized I was expanding, not necessarily losing. Expansions can be so drastic that they feel disorienting. A new facet of me was arriving. One I had to meet and embrace and get to know. I was going through an incredible change, but that didn't mean other parts of me were being replaced.

Allow yourself to become, to expand. Don't feed the temptation to replace your selves. Expand your self. Don't be afraid of all these parts of you. Welcome the mother in you even as you are overwhelmed by her responsibilities. Welcome the achiever in you instead of rejecting her as soulless. Welcome the sensual in you instead of demonizing pleasure. Welcome the artist in you instead of believing she must be defunct now that you are running a household. We are both complete *and* becoming. Let yourself expand.

I keep wondering if one of the things God had in mind when he put Adam and Eve in the garden was giving them a space where they had the freedom to explore, experience, enjoy. I keep wondering if this is how God created us: to give things a whirl, to experiment with different ideas of who and what we might want to do and be, and to allow ourselves to expand exponentially.

Letting myself expand is a divine letting go. Allowing myself to become more, welcoming those shifts and shake-ups is about something of great wonder. I guess I've tried to squeeze my identity into some very tight boxes. Boxes about what it meant to be good, loved, to belong. And instead of judging all this—which I am prone to do—expanding is about welcoming even the boxes I chose and seeing that we are always, in our very feeble and flawed ways, trying to heal ourselves.

Do not fall into the trap of having to narrowly define yourself. You are not a brand, an image, or a product. You are an ever-expanding self, a Created You, which is infinite in its iterations.

The same landscape looks different depending on the light— none of which is truer than the others. A thousand different looks, all of which are poetry.

Reflection & Expression

Have you rejected, left behind, forgotten parts of yourself that may want or need to be reclaimed? Make a list of the different "selves" that go into creating your whole self. For example, your mother self, athlete self, artist self, etc.

If you had four hours to do anything you wanted to do, what would you do?

For Your Brazen Board

Find an image that represents one or more of the many selves that make up who you are.

12

Replace the Fig Leaves

The LORD God made garments of skin for Adam and his wife and clothed them.

—Genesis 3:21 NIV

It's easy to feel loved when you're riding high, performing well, on top of your game. It's more difficult to access those feelings of worthiness and unconditional acceptance when things have gone awry and your humanity is poking out of every seam.

Today I woke up feeling like the Soul Bullies had me cornered. I hate how this comes out of nowhere. Last week the preschool was trying to get in touch with me and I missed their call(s) because the ringer on my phone was turned off. The whole situation resolved, thanks to the rescue efforts of Tina, who ended up having to go to the preschool and take my child home with her until I could be reached. I felt embarrassed and low. I'd let go of it, so I thought, until it was time to show my face at the preschool again this morning and my mind immediately started rehearsing all the reasons why I was unfit for duty.

I was reminded of the two party invitations that slipped through the cracks and the emails I'm behind on. I could feel the Soul Bullies closing in, and then I spilled my coffee everywhere . . . because when the bullies are coming for you, you feel rattled and shaky.

As I was paper-toweling coffee from the counter to the trash can, I remembered one of the all-time most helpful concepts in the universe: sometimes we just need to begin again. Because, we really, truly don't arrive. We just return to the truth. I had to remember to treat myself with care and compassion. I had to remember to breathe. I had to remember to reach out and ask God to remind me that my lovability is not contingent on how well I execute the logistics of life.

And God reminded me of something important, essential even: I am never more loved than in the moment of my failings, my faltering, my humanity. I'm never more loved than the moment when it all falls apart. I turn on myself when things crash—especially if the crash happens on my watch—but God doesn't. He doesn't turn on me—ever. In fact, the total opposite, he wants to love me through my Come Apart if I'll let him.

(Ugghhh, it's practically impossible to tolerate that kind of persistent grace.)

Through God, we've been offered a love that is based solely on someone loving us, totally divested of anything we bring to the table. We're loved, even when we're average, unorganized, plagued, tired, ineffective, worried, and/or totally unspectacular. It's radical, isn't it? Radical, I think, because so many of us have a warped experience of love.

Some of us, having needed to feel loved, believed that letting someone say or do anything they wanted to us would help them love us more. But it just doesn't work that way, does it? Instead, we ended up giving away parts of ourselves. When we do this, we end up feeling less lovable. And the other person ends up taking, taking, taking . . . because we're willing to give ourselves to their bottomless appetite. We relinquish our power to a monger.

I was watching *Top Chef*, and one of the contestants revealed that her parents had never told her they were proud of her. They simply told her as she was going on the show, "Just don't make yourself look bad." Which means, of course, if you read between the lines, "Just don't make *us* look bad." She had made it to the top three and was saying, in an on-camera interview, that if she made it to the finale, then maybe her parents would tell her they were proud of her. How many people grew up with a performance-based version of love? If you are good enough, then you will be accepted. No wonder it's hard to accept God's love.

One of the most courageous things we can do is stare down this love God is offering us and ask ourselves if we really, truly believe it's real. Do you believe you are loved like that? In your worst moments, in your deepest doubts, in your greatest failures, when the preschool can't get hold of you . . . are you loved? Every single day, we each must get up and answer that question for ourselves. Because the way we answer that question really does affect everything.

This is a perfect practice for our twenty minutes of soul time. Simply asking ourselves, in the presence of God, "Do I believe God loves me today?" and then observing what surfaces.

I absolutely love this idea from David Benner, that "God's deepest desire for us is to replace our fig leaves with garments of durability and beauty."[1] I think this is one of the deepest longings of our heart: that we could shed our false protections and believe the God-in-us is enough. Our false attachments, our clinging to cover, help us forget about our nakedness. God doesn't want us to cover our own nakedness. He wants us to turn to him in our vulnerability and allow him to robe us, clothe us in his love.

My friend Elaine told me recently, "I love every version of you."

Have you ever had someone look you in the eye and tell you that? The night before I had been ranting about something, started ugly crying, and the next day I started grabbing for the fig leaves. I felt embarrassed that I had let her see me like that, in a state that felt out of control, snotty. She offered me something I couldn't offer myself: No condemnation. Unconditional love. She reminded me that my garments are made of durability and beauty, and I do not need to shroud myself in shame.

God does the very same thing for us. He reaches toward us and says, "I love every version of you, you gorgeous thing."

We can put those words on like the gown they are, and whisper, "Sorry, shame. I am ready to live wildly loved."

Reflection & Expression

Thank you, God, for loving me even when I am _____

_____.

For Your Brazen Board

Find an image of love. Or write the phrase "wildly loved" somewhere on your board.

Add the phrase "I love every version of you."

13

Fall in Love

Usually, when the distractions of daily life deplete our energy, the first thing we eliminate is the thing we need the most: quiet, reflective time. Time to dream, time to contemplate what's working and what's not, so that we can make changes for the better.

—Sarah Ban Breathnach

I have been struggling internally with my own need for creative expression and the forms that expression wants to take. I believe so entirely in letting myself run free creatively, but then, when it comes to certain forms of this expression—like in my home, for example—sometimes it feels frivolous. That's the word that jumped out of my mouth, anyway, when I was talking to Beth-with-Dreads.

I told her how much of a dilemma I'd been feeling around my home: feeling restless, wanting to make some changes, moving toward those changes, getting paralyzed, and then frustratingly dropping the entire enterprise. Only to have the whole longing resurface, this time with more energy behind it. This is the cycle.

I brought all this up to Beth because she helps guide me through my internal tensions, and she said, "Why do you feel you need to stop yourself from thinking about making changes to your home?"

And without thinking, the following tumbles out: "Because it's frivolous."

Her eyes open significantly wider as she says, "And frivolous is a bad thing?"

"Yes, obviously," I say back.

And now I'm caught in her trap.

"Leeana, I wonder if this is the word that might lead you home. I wonder," Beth continues, "if you might spend some time with the word *frivolous* and see what you find out. I think there's something that needs to be honored here."

"Oh Beth," I want to say, smiling, "would it be OK if I punched you?"

At first I assumed she was making way too big a deal out of the word. I just spit it out. It wasn't like it was the real truth or anything. But I decided I would spend some time with "frivolous" just to appease her.

During my next twenty minutes of soul time, I wrote "frivolous" at the top of my legal pad, and I made a list of things that felt frivolous and, also, desirous. The entire exercise seemed simultaneously dumb and important.

I look up *frivolous* in the dictionary and find the definitions that seem to be saying something to me: "silly, trifling, empty, worthless, broken, crumbled, of little weight or importance, so clearly insufficient."[1]

And then I hear this question: "Leeana, do you feel that *you* are frivolous?" And I wonder if this is the question all along. I can't participate in frivolous things because it might mean I am silly, empty, worthless, of little weight or importance.

I look up more synonyms and definitions: "not having any serious purpose or value, irrelevant, jokey, foolish, superficial, shallow."

When I read the word *irrelevant*, I feel as though I've been hit. Isn't that one of my greatest fears? I have a friend who told me that her whole life she has felt "adjunct," which means "useful, but not necessary." Pardon me while I break out in hives.

What is so necessary to me about having this sense of gravitas, legitimacy, relevance? Do I believe something I could do or produce will deliver the belief for me and others that I am weighty and important?

I look up more synonyms and definitions: "self-indulgently carefree, unconcerned about or lacking any serious purpose."

And here's where things got kind of weird.

When I was in graduate school, I had a choice between a program in creative writing and one in literature. I chose literature because, obviously, people don't become writers. That's ridiculous. People become teachers. That's what real adults do. I chose the practical choice; the one that I believed was more legitimate, perhaps.

But not only that. I also chose the path that seemed safer, more doable. A sure bet. Looking back, I wonder if I shut down a piece of myself to make that decision. I wonder if it ever occurred to me that I could pursue whatever I wanted to, and that I couldn't make a wrong decision in that moment.

Somewhere along the way, that inventive little girl inside me got inoculated with the belief that she could create, but it better have a purpose. It better not be frivolous. Because I must, at all costs, avoid being irrelevant. You're probably way ahead of me on this; when we work out of this place, we are working to secure what we already have and what will never be delivered to us through our productivity.

I keep reading more about *frivolous*. Its origin is around 1425–1475, and it comes from late Middle English meaning "to crumble."[2]

unworthy of serious attention

trivial

inappropriately silly

not serious or sensible in content, attitude, or behavior

unworthy of serious or sensible treatment

unimportant

not worthy of serious notice

superficial

pointless

minor

Some of us have staked our sense of self on whatever it takes to "not crumble." We're hooked into the need to know that what we're saying, doing, offering matters. It's our worst fear to be unworthy of serious attention. Until one day we realize how exhausting it is to strive so relentlessly. We hear God's whisper:

"Leeana, what if you stopped trying to be so worthy? What if you stopped focusing on your relevance? What if you stopped trying to secure your own meaningfulness? What if you let yourself crumble?"

Um, no thanks. But just for fun . . . how?

"Be frivolous, again and again. Dabble in the garden I have given you. What do you love?" Hmmm, well . . .

I love the winter beach

I love fires in the fireplace

I love boots

I love ideas

I love feeling inspired

I love feeling decisive

I love naps

I love humor

I love texture

I love interesting clothes

I love space

I love rural France

I love being lost in my own world

I love being deeply connected

I love eating charcuterie outside in the summer

I love being on a team

I love the names Delphine and Valentina

I love a Christmas baby

I love Steve's skin

I love green eyes

I love chips and salsa

I love the Chargers

I love bougainvillea

I love fuchsia and aqua

I love pea gravel

I love a fountain

I love black and white

I love laughing with my family

I love Scrabble

I love an earthy, tobacco-y red wine

I love crab legs

I love metallics

I love kraft paper

I love ceviche with lots of acid

I love a rib eye like Steve makes it

I love my vanilla perfume

I love galvanized metal

I love hot showers

I love black bikinis

I love white interiors

I love faux fur

I love *Project Runway*

I love getting lost (or found) in a book

I love the rain

I love poetry

I love henna

I love tennis

I love documentaries on famous chefs

I love Northern California

I love, I love, I love . . .

"Run toward what you love with unapologetic abandon.
Fall in love with your life, Leeana, instead of trying to make

something of it. You already have everything you've ever wanted. Now go enjoy it."

This is the whisper that penetrates my soul.

And then I wonder, What if it's true? What if I lived into the "already" of my life, and spent more time and energy exploring the garden I've been given? What if I sat in the center of what I have and asked God to show me what is already here, for my pleasure? What if I were free? What if I *am* free?

Does this feel too good to be true? Way too frivolous to be possible?

"Go, Leeana, go. Go to the studio of your soul. Slip off your big turquoise ring and put it in the beautiful bowl by the stack of canvases. Climb into your overalls. Put your hands in all the vibrant paints and play. Get lost in the garden I've already given you. You have everything you need.

"I'm here . . . waiting for you."

Reflection & Expression

Make a list of outings or activities that seem frivolous to you and yet would fill you up.

What have you *already* been given?

For Your Brazen Board

Include an image of something you love.

Add something you deem "frivolous."

Part Two

Reclaim

{YOUR VOICE}

14

Be the Mermaid with a Megaphone

The most courageous act is still to think for yourself. Aloud.

—Coco Chanel

I was in World Market last week, and I was drawn to this display of journals. The one that immediately caught my eye has a mermaid on the cover. She has her right hand on her hip and her left hand is holding a megaphone up to her mouth. She's cutting her eyes toward you as you hold the journal, and she looks generally like she's about to kick butt in her powder blue eyeshadow and pink and blue tail.

I love her. And at the risk of sounding like a total narcissist, the longer I look at her, the more I think she kind of looks like me. Or I look like her. I can see my eyes in her eyes. I can see my nose in her nose. I can see my lips in her lips.

I can see the brazen me in her, and something about her is daring me.

Graffiti artwork surrounds her. In fact, she's composed entirely of mixed media graffiti, and I notice that on her neck—maybe where her voice box is located—there's a small circle with an X in it. As if to say, "Right here. X marks the spot."

Tumbling out of her megaphone are the following words of Anaïs Nin:

> I have no
> FEAR
> of depths
> and a
> GREAT
> FEAR of
> SHALLOW
> living.

My daughter Lane has been an especially beautiful toddler and little girl, and I have often had people, strangers, stop and tell me so. When she was four, we were playing at the park and two men approached her, wanting to take her picture. I was immediately uncomfortable with what they were doing. I could feel inside me that they were crossing a boundary. But I could also feel an immediate dis-ease with speaking up.

One of the men was telling her to pose. One of the men was laughing in a way that felt lewd to me.

I froze. A swell of indignation rose up in me, but I choked on the words I intuitively wanted to say. Instead, I heard in my head:

Don't cause a scene. It's just a picture. It's not that big of a deal.

Still, all I wanted to do was scream.

For all the little girls who no one stood up for. For all the lewdness and filth that is in this world. For the objectification. And, probably, for a young Leeana who was screaming from inside me somewhere, asking to be protected, begging for rescue.

But I hesitated.

Then somehow, the voice inside me that is stronger and more primal than the pleaser climbed up and out of my throat and from some primordial place inside my soul I roared, "NO!"

Maybe it was the voice of God, pushing against the core of my being, reminding me that I am a strong mother, I am a soulful mother. Even with my heart pounding and my hands sweating, I can spread my wings and protect, and it does not matter what the predators of this world think of me. Not for one second.

"NO. NO. NO. You cannot take a picture of her. NO. Please leave. Get away from her. NO. NO. NO." I flung my arms into the air, shooing the wolves from my baby bird.

And they looked at me with such disgust. Such annoyance. Like I was nothing. Like I had no right to tell them NO. They smirked, looking me up and down, as if I were the biggest joke. And then they finally left.

I wanted to sob. Not because of how they looked at me—though it still makes me want to claw their eyes out—but because I almost didn't say anything. How many times in my life have I chosen to stay quiet? Chosen to appear nonthreatening? Chosen to keep the peace? Chosen to placate and please and pretend none of it bothered me instead of saying, "NO. NO you cannot. NO I will not. NO it's not OK"?

You can't tiptoe into your voice. Whether you're whispering or you're shouting, you use it or you don't. Kinda like a megaphone. Once in a while we have to turn some tables on behalf of those God has put in our hands. Not to make a spectacle for the sake of a spectacle but because one of our spiritual obligations in this world is to be a voice for the voiceless, even if the voiceless is the little girl locked inside us.

Remember, we have been given dominion, charge, and if we are hedging and shrinking we will not be practicing dominion in the ways God has called us to. Reclaiming our voice is about letting the freedom crawl up and out of us in a way that is congruent with our becoming.

It's a tragedy, an unmitigated tragedy, that some of us didn't have anyone who picked up the megaphone on our behalf. And we still don't. The only thing I know to do is to start telling the truth, and start becoming that strong voice we wish *we* would have had when we were young. I am raising three young children, two of whom are girls, and I consider it one of my greatest honors to walk beside them as they find their one-of-a-kind wild in this world. What's insanely true, however, is that for me to help them know their voices, I must know mine.

Hiding can look like a thousand different postures and performances, but one of the most egregious is swallowing down our own God-breathed strength.

Reflection & Expression

What are three lies you're currently telling yourself and others? What are three truths you'd like to be sharing with the people in your world? Your sentences might start this way:

I will no longer . . .
I will begin to . . .

Reflect on a time when you needed someone to stand up for you and they didn't.

For Your Brazen Board

Find an image of someone using their voice.

15

Yell for the Ball

No memory of having starred
Atones for later disregard
Or keeps the end from being hard.

—Robert Frost

The only time I remember feeling afraid on the volleyball court was my first tournament as a high school freshman. I had made the varsity team, and we were in Palm Springs for the first matches of the season.

We were playing in a huge gym with courts set up everywhere, whistles blowing in all directions. Our setter set me the ball, and I heard a whistle blow. So I caught the ball. What became clear—after everyone stood looking at me with incredulity and annoyance—was that the whistle had come from a different court.

One of my teammates actually yelled, "What are you *doing*?!?!" I stuttered my way through an explanation and the game went on.

I hid in the bathroom after the match and cried.

This is the perfect illustration of one of my greatest fears in life: you get the set—it's your turn to shine!—and there you are holding the ball when you're supposed to be hitting it. Looking like the world's biggest idiot. Everyone else knows what to do, except you. All of this happening with a crowd looking on.

I don't remember feeling unsure of myself on the volleyball court after that. Something in me clicked or switched and I never questioned myself again. I had a club coach my junior year of high school who screamed at me in front of a gym full of people, and I remember being furious, but not embarrassed. I remember how red-faced he would get, how he would throw chairs. And I remember proving him wrong about me.

By the time I played college volleyball, I always wanted the ball. Shamelessly. I was a team player, and had no problem with others getting the ball too. But if the game was on the line, I was comfortable knowing the ball was coming to me. I might have even preferred it when the game was in my hands.

I look back at that me, and I admire her. I admire her strength, her assurance, her resilience, her work ethic, her self-confidence. Maybe most of all, I admire how she trusted the competence she had worked hard to earn.

Since college, I have become increasingly wary of myself. I went through a difficult relationship in graduate school, right out of college. I look at the Leeana in that relationship—reduced, scared, scraping—and she is a million miles from the Leeana of the volleyball court days.

I think about myself today and my vocation as mother and wife and maker, and I often spend more time questioning myself than I do cheering for myself. I think about that Leeana in college, full of an inner confidence, hungry for opportunity, and I know my days would be far more fulfilling if I could recapture more of her fire.

Recently, someone asked me what I do for a living. Whenever this question comes up, I feel a fluttery anxiety inside. Like I'm holding the ball, and everyone's looking at me. I feel the need to hedge, to hide, for some crazy reason. I don't want to worry about perceived expectations or judgments, and so it's far easier to play small instead of own up to something that feels vulnerable.

I don't think it should be lost on me that the first human beings hid when they did not know what else to do. When they were afraid and confused and ashamed of how vulnerable they felt, their first instinct was to hide.

When we feel exposed, we hide. It seems practically primal, right? We cover ourselves and duck and play small to keep from being hurt. We hide because something in us feels threatened, embarrassed, unsure. It's a defense mechanism, inborn in every creature on the planet.

I get that we hide. It's a thing. But why am I hiding? What am I afraid of? Why aren't I yelling for the ball?

Then I hear, "Leeana, you're not sure how to define success, and so you are afraid to claim your calling until you know for sure you are successful at it. But here's what I want you to think about: Your calling isn't an experiment. It's not a 'well, we'll see how it goes.' It's an imprint I put on you, a way I have created you, the channel to your soul, the beauty I want to share with the world through you. Because of all that, it's also very vulnerable."

How do you own something fully while also releasing the results fully? How do you own your calling while not making that ownership contingent on your arbitrary definition of success?

Believing in yourself is vulnerable. Really vulnerable. It would be so much easier to believe in myself if Oprah called me and asked me to be on her network. Right? Well, that's actually an interesting assumption: When the success comes, then I'll know this is what I'm supposed to do. When the success comes, that will be my confirmation to step into my work more fully. When the success comes, then I'll feel great about myself and my work. Right?

In her podcast, "Magic Lessons," I heard Elizabeth Gilbert say these right-on words: "Any talent that we have but do not use becomes a burden." We are lugging something around in our souls that was meant to be released, given away, not harbored. So many of you know what I'm talking about here. You're carrying the burden of a story unwritten, a point of view unexpressed, a world unmade. Maybe, just maybe, it's your turn.

Sometimes the most brazen thing we can do is shut up. But sometimes, the most brazen thing we can do is yell for the ball.

Reflection & Expression

What area of your life feels vulnerable right now? When do you feel tempted to hide?

For Your Brazen Board

Find an image that represents you trusting your competence.

16

Cheer for the Chargers

Dwell in possibility.
—Emily Dickinson

I grew up watching the San Diego Chargers and have become really attached to them. Unfortunately for me, they are streaky and hard to watch and will break your heart season after everloving season. AND YET, I keep coming back for more.

Sure, I could adopt Steve's childhood team, the 49ers. I could root for my mom's beloved Saints. But it doesn't feel right. I love my Chargers. And if there were ever a sign that I love an underdog more than any other human in this world, it is the fact that I will always get excited for football season because THIS YEAR my Chargers are going to do it. They're going to win it all. I just know it.

This thing in me that loves the Chargers is the same thing in me that loves the Seattle Seahawks' Super Bowl–winning quarterback, Russell Wilson. Or at least I love his story. He's shorter than the prototypical NFL quarterback, and everyone overlooked him because of it. Scouts, pundits, and coaches all bet against him in the draft. And he's proven every one of them wrong. Like, embarrassingly wrong.

I love a comeback story more than anyone else in the world. I love a Cinderella team in March Madness. I'll watch televised fencing just to witness an upset. I absolutely love it when something happens that everyone said couldn't. I love it when what's on paper doesn't dictate reality. I love it when we sit and stare at the TV because we just beheld something that everyone assured us was against all odds.

Every time I start to feel cynical about this world, just plop me down in front of an athletic competition and I will immediately be reminded of how much I love to hope, especially when that hope is ill-advised.

Lately, I've been thinking a lot about our wounds and our wonder, our humanity and our divinity. I've been thinking about this, likely because I've been through an extended season of in-your-face humanity, when I needed to welcome and make peace with my utter humanness. And then honor it. The wounded, flawed, limited, skulking, limping part of me.

Good grief.

I've had to turn toward the Hard and get help. I've had to turn toward my need for rest and sit the heck down. I've had to bring in the borders of my life, which is painful and very inconvenient to many others. I've likely disappointed people and have needed to accept that if disappointing others was the cost for my own recovery, then I would have to learn to be OK with letting others down. I've had to focus, for a season, on getting better in many, many ways. This is the kind of work we wonder if we'll ever emerge from. Will life ever feel light again? Will there ever be ease? Will I ever have energy again?

I would have never, ever thought I'd say what I'm about to say next, BUT . . . as difficult as this past season has been, the hard lesson of learning to walk with myself like a companion instead of a critic has been a season of grace. God has revealed to me in large and small ways the parts of my life that were not working, the ways in which I was not living congruent with my own soul, and my subsequent hiding.

You plunge into these seasons of recovery because of trauma or a rock-bottom experience, and then you have to crawl. The whole journey is so slow. Then one day you realize you've re-emerged into the light.

I believe God wants us to make peace with our woundedness, and that is exactly the journey I've been on. What's more, I believe God also wants us to make peace with our wonder, which is the journey I'm starting into. We need to welcome our brokenness, but also our belovedness. This is the brazen path.

Someone recently told me that one of her definitions of maturity is the ability to hold seeming opposites in tension. She called it a "kingdom value." God holds the tension of humanity and divinity through the incarnation, and he invites us to do that same holding: fully embracing the wounds and fully embracing the wonder.

The word *wonder* is both a verb—"to wonder"—and a noun, originating from words meaning "marvelous thing, miracle, object of astonishment."

Because that, my friends, is who we really are, before the world got to us. Before our parents broke our hearts. Before we were violated. Before we were screamed at. Before we were told we were stupid. Before we started relying on substances to deal with our pain. Before a partner stole something from us we didn't intend to give. Before the church told us to quietly make the coffee. Before all that . . . before the anger and the

sadness and the chaos and the fear and the shame and the regret
. . . before all that, beneath all that, there is a Created Center,
a miracle, a marvelous thing. Creation!

And we don't believe it's enough because it's not of this world.

So we cover it up and deny it and quiet it because it's scary,
it's untamed, it's brazen. We let other people—people who
fear that part of us—convince us we should stay small. And
we settle for a cheap substitute: image. When God has gifted
us with something that is so much bigger and wider and deeper
than image ever could be: identity.

I spent a bit of time listening to myself and to God on the
subject of wonder the other day. I went outside and here is what
I heard:

> *God:* Leeana, it is time to shift from wounds to wonder.
> Life has an ebb and flow, seasons. And the season
> that you're entering is a season of focusing on
> your wonder. It is time to lay down what has been
> heavy and pick up what is light. It is time to get to
> know your Created Center. It is time to welcome
> the wonder in yourself.
>
> What about you needs to be celebrated, hon-
> ored? What are you unnecessarily editing?
>
> *Leeana:* God, what wonder do you see in me?

And you'll never guess what I heard.

> *God:* Hope. Hope is a part of your wonder. You are
> not a cynic. You are a believer. You believe people
> can heal. You believe beauty matters. You believe
> creating matters. You believe things could change.
> You believe the Chargers can win the Super Bowl,
> for crying out loud. This is all hope.

Leeana: God, how do I cultivate hope?

   God: You use your hopeful voice. Don't edit it. Don't apologize for it. Don't downplay it. Don't silence it.

I'm a hoper. And, apparently, according to God, hope is a part of my wonder. Who knew? So if I'm understanding all this correctly, I think I'm supposed to honor my hope-ness, celebrate it, let it out, put my strong voice toward hope. The world is full of cynics and critics and naysayers and not-gonna-happeners. Negativity is tired, if you ask me. It's way too easy to stand back and poke holes in anything and everything. There are gifts for the participant in life, while the only gift the critic holds is his own opinions and his own well-crafted image.

Sure, hope opens you up to disappointment. But I think I'm fairly convinced I'd rather be hopeful than hidden.

I think everyone's wonder is somewhat similar and somewhat different. It's the thing the world needs from you. It's the thing you long to give but have perhaps shut down or shut up for some reason. It's precious to you and might make you tear up if you think about it too long. It's the part of you the world didn't get its hands on. It's your Created Center, and it's worth rescuing, reclaiming, returning to.

Reflection & Expression

Ask:

God, what wonder do you see in me?

God, how do I cultivate my wonder?

God, how do I honor my wonder?

God, what wonder in me do I need to voice?

What is something about YOU that you appreciate?

For Your Brazen Board

Find an image, color, texture, item that represents your wonder. Write the word *WONDER* somewhere on your board.

17

Do Not Eat
the Rotten Chicken

The very nature of marriage means saying yes before you know what it will cost. Though you may say the "I do" of the wedding ritual in all sincerity, it is the testing of that vow over time that makes you married.

—Kathleen Norris, *Acedia & me*

I don't know about you, but one of the ways my hiding has manifested itself is in some of my long-haul relationships. At times, I would rather keep the peace than speak up for myself or on behalf of what I'm feeling. When you're in a relationship for the marathon, not the sprint, you have to be wise. You have to pick your battles. We all know this. But you also have to be careful about getting lost. About letting yourself become voiceless. Especially if you, like me, are married to one of the most intense human beings on the planet.

Steve and I have been married almost twelve years as of this writing. In the last few years, I've been practicing using my voice in our relationship. Here's an example of how that's gone for us:

One of the ways Steve expresses his creativity and care for all of us is through food. Braised, smoked, roasted, brined, marinated, seared food. Natural, whole, seasoned, delicious food. He wraps his arms around you with this food that seems to be offered from his very soul.

On this particular day, as he began cooking the chicken he'd been brining for the last 24 hours, a death-smell began filling our house.

"I think the chicken's bad," I say to Steve.

"No it's not. It's fine," he contends.

"No really, it smells like Jonestown in here. I think you should throw it out."

"I don't want to talk about it," he says, and completely shuts me down.

But, of course, I can't leave it alone: "We don't have to talk about it, but I am not eating that chicken. The kids are not eating that chicken. And I certainly hope you don't eat that chicken because I don't want to have to take you to the emergency room in the middle of the night for botulism just because you were too prideful to admit THE CHICKEN IS ROTTEN."

"I said, I don't want to talk about it."

He won't look at me. He continues to cook the chicken— literally begins searing it in the cast iron pan—and the smell is getting so bad that at one point Luke and Lane come into the kitchen and say, "Dad, Dad, the whole house smells like a giant stinky."

He keeps cooking.

Did I mention we had dinner guests who were observing this entire fiasco as it unfolded? (One of whom, OF COURSE, is a marriage and family therapist. UGGHHH.)

And the house not only smelled of rotten poultry, it was also filled with eggshells that we were all required to walk on as Steve said to me, practically hissing as I hovered aggressively over the entire scene, "Do not say one word."

Things went on like this for what felt like . . . all of history. Steve silently cooking rotten chicken, fuming. Me, hovering and snorting and feeling confident that I needed to reiterate over and over again: I. Will. Not. Eat. That. Chicken.

Steve had invested thirty-six hours in this moment. Making the brine. Letting the free range, hormone free, very expensive whole chicken swim its little heart out in that brine. He was not going to give up so easily. He could not figure out what went wrong, since he had done this same brine in the past and it had turned out beautifully. He could not come to terms with the fact that the chicken was ruined. So he just kept cooking it. Despite the very obvious evidence, because Steve could not figure out how the chicken had rotted, it was not yet officially rotten.

In the end, he realized the brine water was a little too warm and it caused the chicken to go bad in its overnight bath. He later told me that he just needed some time to figure out what had gone wrong and, too, that he was mad the chicken was inedible.

Here's the truth about finding your voice in relationships: it's a mess. We overcompensate for the ways we've been quiet in the past. We let all our big feelings out. It's like the Wild West: Who can draw first?

Sometimes speaking up goes beautifully, but often it doesn't. We have to be ready to deal with the aftermath of standing toe-to-toe with someone we do life with. Often the people we have the most history with can be the very same people with whom we have fallen into certain communication patterns. We call a spade a spade, we point out that the emperor is in fact not wearing any clothes, and all of this truth-telling isn't particularly appreciated.

The trick is learning to be assertive with our voice without being destructive. Learning to be direct without being damaging. Maturity is about speaking our truth with grace, about showing up but not being a bully about it. That's hard, right? We tend to swing the pendulum from one extreme to another—silence or outburst.

We went out to dinner with some dear friends sometime after the fight, and the incident came up again at the restaurant. We literally rehashed the entire episode to them, including getting mad at each other all over again. Thankfully, Eric and Kara were unfazed by the reenactment and were able to endure our intensity.

Normally conflict makes me anxious, and I would have started laughing in this tinny nervous laugh and I would have tried my best to wriggle us out of the conversation and talk about something easier. But I didn't. I let us get mad at each other all over again. At one point, I even got up and went to the bathroom because I wanted to punch Steve.

I don't think this is always healthy—to rehash and rehash and rehash. But in this case, it was good for me to hang in there with the discomfort, to show up in the conflict, to not let something go that was truly bothering me, to be honest about the ways I felt unheard.

Last week, Steve braised pork belly for Ken's birthday. He worked on it for hours, and the smell of the fresh herbs and marbled pork filled our house with an aroma like heaven.

He transported our Dutch oven to Ken and Elaine's house and finished cooking it in their oven while we ate bacon-wrapped dates and drank a special bottle of wine we got on a trip together last year to Napa. The aroma began to fill *their* house with warmth too.

When the pork belly was done, Steve took the lid off and served Ken and Elaine, Leo and Kerry, and me. Everyone oohed and aahed at this love letter in a cast iron pot, which got me thinking again about the rotten chicken.

When the chicken went south, it was about more than just the chicken (isn't it always?). It was about a missed opportunity to feed people in the way Steve had intended. A missed opportunity to care for people in the way he had planned. And I came barreling in, in the middle of all that frustration, and started stomping on his toes. He hissed back. Mainly, I think, because I was running roughshod over something sacred to him.

Every single one of us has a relationship or two where we've had to learn the fine art of knowing when to push back and knowing when to shut up. We've had to do the delicate and courageous work of standing up for ourselves. We've had to learn how to navigate the aftermath too.

Steve and I were both trying to make the other person understand something on that rotten chicken day. And in our efforts to try to get the other person to understand, we missed each other. I never want my needing to find my voice to cost Steve his soul. And I never want Steve needing to express his soul to cost me my voice.

Because, here's what I know for a fact: the voice and the soul are a brazen combination.

Reflection & Expression

Reflect on a relationship where you have trouble speaking up.

Finish this sentence for yourself:

I need to speak up about _____.

For Your Brazen Board

Find a picture that represents the assertive you.

18

Make Peace with Self-Possession

It takes courage to grow up and become who you really are.

—e. e. cummings

"What would it be like for you to disappoint someone?" Elaine asks me when I tell her I'm in a couple of churn-worthy situations I'd like to crawl out of. (Ummmm, please stop asking me such aggressive questions, Elaine.)

My eyes dart and my mouth drops open slightly. I take a deep breath, knowing I don't have a good answer to her question.

Have you ever been in a situation where someone was crossing your boundaries and it was making you churn? Maybe this person overstayed their welcome at your house. Maybe they wanted more of your time than you wanted to give. Maybe they had expectations of you that you did not want to fulfill. Maybe you made a decision about something and they bulldozed right over your decision. Maybe they walked right into your house and took over, when you had not asked them to take over.

I've been in a few of these highly awkward, usually angering, situations. I've had to learn the hard way that sometimes people feel entitled to you, your time, your home, your friendship, even though you have not given them passage. What frustrates me the most in these situations is that I either have to be uncomfortable or, to alleviate the discomfort, reinforce my boundary. I resent being put in the position of having to be the "bad guy."

But, wouldn't you know, that's part of being a grown-up. (Hideous.)

We can take the precious time and energy we have and spend it churning, or we can spend that same precious time and energy creating, communing, cooking, cuddling. The only thing standing in our way? Possibly having to tell someone no and then living with their disappointment in us. Which is kind of a lot to deal with, if you ask me.

I understand in theory the idea that I will have to cross people in this world, especially the people who are not listening to my words, not heeding my decisions, not respecting my space. But for so long I've never called people out on these things because *I was more concerned with being thought well of than protecting my own wellness.* Then all of a sudden I realized I was tired not because life was full but because life was full of things that were draining the soul right out of me.

My arms are wide. A certain side of me is highly invested in wooing (winning others over), if I let it off the leash. All of these things are giantly beneficial in life when you're trying to build new relationships or trying to make easy conversation or trying to make an uncomfortable situation comfortable or even trying to persuade someone over to your way of thinking.

Most of the time, this all works out great. But then sometimes I am caught in my own woo-gone-wrong moment, and I realize I cannot tolerate asserting my needs and my boundaries for fear someone will think poorly of me. So I obliterate my limits, and give someone entry, even though I can already feel the low rumbles of the churn.

I know all this sounds terribly adolescent. It is, really. It's the adolescent in me that is looking to secure her spot through affability and approachability. It is the adolescent in me who never disappointed, who worked to be sure she never, ever disappointed.

But I am older now. I care more about living from a soulful place than a striving place. I'd like to settle into my own skin a bit more than the adolescent me ever did. She leaned heavy on applause, and she got it, but I'm ready for something more than acceptance at this stage of my life. I'm longing to be self-possessed.

When you think of a person who is self-possessed, think about someone who knows what she believes, knows her own opinions, knows her own taste, and isn't trying to morph or chameleon into what the next person walking toward her needs her to be. She has a sense of herself and she lives true to that sense, honoring it.

She has a strength of intuition, and she's loyal to her Created Center. She can practice her "no" with confidence because she's in tune with her own needs, her family's needs, her soul's needs, and she isn't going to allow the requests of others to bulldoze her priorities and her capacity.

And if someone manages to get close to her and then they abuse that closeness, she is able to rescue herself. She's able to stand up for her own existence and politely excuse herself from the relationship. If the other person thinks she's a heartless witch for doing so, that's fine. Because the self-possessed woman knows, surely, that she is not a heartless witch. She is, in fact, a soul warrior.

She has spent extended periods of time in the presence of God, listening to the deep-waters voice of God that teaches her to honor her family, honor her craft, honor her desires, honor what has been put in her hands. She knows she is God-possessed, and so she is able to be confidently self-possessed.

Her limits and her boundaries aren't just a "no" to intruders. They are about protecting her "deeper yes," the yes she has fought to discover in the presence of God. Her creative space. Her quiet mornings. Her kids' bedtime. Her night out with her husband. Her sanity. The self-possessed woman is learning that a well-tended life requires these touchstones, and she will be angry if she allows other people's agendas for her to rob her of her life rhythm.

Sometimes I find myself angry with the offending party. Don't they know they're crossing my boundaries? Don't they know that's too much to ask? Don't they know that's not going to work for me? All my energy is directed at the other person when I'm actually really frustrated with me. When I refuse to rescue myself from the boundary bulldozers, I'm choosing to keep everyone happy with me instead of live my own truth. This is me silencing my own voice, refusing to be the soul warrior I want to be. This is me being others-possessed, not self-possessed, for a self-possessed person takes responsibility for herself and her life.

I'm just now learning it's OK to say . . .

I don't know.

I don't like that.

I don't want that.

I can't do that.

I need help.

I need to think about it.

I'm not sure.

I don't think that will work for me.

I need to go now.

No, thank you.

No, you can't.

In other words, I'm just now learning how to articulate—out loud—inconvenient truths. Not to be rigid or jerky just for the sake of getting in people's faces—belligerence is every bit as adolescent as people pleasing—but to protect those things that matter most to me. Exhibit A:

I was at a party once when I was nine months pregnant with Elle. A guy, who was falling down drunk, kept flirting with me, inching his way closer and closer to me. I was disastrously uncomfortable. Steve was way on the other side of the very noisy room, not privy to my discomfort. I looked up across the room, waiting for him to rescue me, not realizing I had everything it took to rescue myself.

The man scooted closer, invading my personal space. He leaned in to tell me something closer to my face and he ran right into my huge belly, which was apparently the first time he realized I was, *ahem*, already spoken for.

He looked up at me, alarmed, and he backed away, out the door to the patio, and promptly fell in the pool.

Why couldn't I protect my own dignity in that situation? Why did I let him get close enough to run into my belly in the first place? Why did I give him that kind of power?

Not anymore.

So we decide to build the boundary muscle and we violently swing the pendulum of petulance over to the other side of things and we start yelling at anyone who will listen, usually our partner (see earlier confessions on the subject of rotten chicken). We start standing up for ourselves in knee-jerk protests that are unproductive and unhelpful.

And, ultimately, even if we learn how to stand up for ourselves in ways that are productive and healthy, that person across the table from us may decide they don't particularly appreciate our newfound liberation and they may decide to stand right up too.

This is not clean-cut.

Beth calls it the "prayer practice of disappointing others," and she gives me this practice as an assignment. I hate what it brings up in me. Even the idea of letting someone down turns my insides to flubber.

But I'll tell you some of the biggest ways we stay in hiding: Worry far more about being liked than being known. Worry far more about wooing others than honoring ourselves. Worry far more about keeping the peace than finding our voice. Worry far more about control than figuring out who we are. This is how we learn to live as a chameleon, and it's no good. Instead, we want to look a lot more like this from *The Velveteen Rabbit*:

> You become. It takes a long time. That's why it doesn't happen often to people who break easily, or have sharp edges, or who have to be carefully kept. Generally, by the time you are Real, most of your hair has been loved off, and your eyes drop out and you get loose in the joints and very shabby. But these things don't matter at all, because once you are Real you can't be ugly, except to people who don't understand.[1]

So where do we start?

We start by talking to God about the "deeper yes" of our lives, asking him to help us discover or rediscover those pursuits and people worth protecting our time and energy for. And then we tell the truth, which is so much harder than I imagined. But you know what's even harder than telling the truth? Looking back and realizing you never quite had the time to really live.

Reflection & Expression

Write about your "deeper yes" or what you'd like to make space for in your life.

For Your Brazen Board

Find an image that represents your "deeper yes."

19

Tell the Truth

Silence becomes cowardice when occasion demands speaking out the whole truth and acting accordingly.

—Mahatma Gandhi

I recently attended a reading by a popular writer. After she talked for an hour about writing and life, she did a brave (or stupid, depending on your perspective) thing. She opened the mic and allowed people to come forward and ask their questions.

These situations trigger my anxiety. My heart starts to beat a little faster and my palms get sweaty. On this day, my hands were sticking to my notes: *People can ask all sorts of ill-advised questions. Doesn't she know that?!? People are going to make this terribly uncomfortable. I mean, unlike quiet and good little me over here, a lot of people are totally inappropriate. Doesn't she know that?!?*

And wouldn't you know, the worst possible thing happened. A young man came forward with papers in his hand and began to talk about how he receives revelation from God and writes it down and had an entire manuscript that came to him as direct dictation from God himself.

(The room is getting twitchy.)

And so because he is God's ghostwriter, he is certain that God has also told him to bring the manuscript to the event and make sure the famous writer receives it because it is destined for publication.

Personally, this kind of stuff gives me hives. And if it would have been me up there in front, receiving this information in real time, I would have done whatever I could to get out of that moment as quickly as possible. This, though, is the weakling in me. I would have taken the manuscript and then never read it and I would have placated the young man just to move things along. I would have hidden behind a lie.

I would make a decision to try to keep everyone comfortable instead of being brave.

The famous writer coolly and kindly told the young man, "I'm so sorry, but I won't be able to take your manuscript. I don't have the time to read it and I would just be taking it and then telling you I will read it when I actually won't."

The young man interrupted her and started pleading and repeating that God himself had told him to come to the event and to make sure she got the manuscript.

She repeated firmly and calmly, "I won't be able to take your manuscript. I do not have the time to read it and I don't want to lie to you."

The room was silent.

I'm not sure what everyone else in the room was feeling in that moment, but I could feel the knot in my sternum go slack.

She was taking charge of a very awkward and uncomfortable moment. She was not allowing herself to be steamrolled. She was not letting this young man be in charge. She was in charge.

I felt so relieved. And then I felt inspired. Because I would have never done what she did. Even though my intuition was to tell that guy to SIT DOWN, I would have played it much safer.

What happens, though, when I put on that plastic smile and I say something I actually don't think, is that I have to then live with *internal* conflict. Conflict with myself. Because I didn't speak up, because I didn't say what I really think.

Steve has this great adage about dealing with conflict. He says, "Hard on the issue; easy on the person."

That is exactly what this writer did. She was very firm on the issue but she did it in a way that was cool, calm, and not degrading. She wasn't a jerk. She was direct. She didn't give this guy—a guy who was taking advantage of a situation in a very uncomfortable way—her power. She didn't let her own personal boundary get crossed. Even with a thousand of us looking on.

Whoa.

Reflection & Expression

Think about a recent conflict. What did you say or do? What did you *want* to say or do?

For Your Brazen Board

Find an image of someone who is expressing her power.

20

Commemorate the Clarity

The time is ripe for trying to figure out where we have come from and where we are going to, for sifting through the things we have done and the things we have left undone for a clue to who we are and who, for better or worse, we are becoming.

—Frederick Buechner

Steve and I have spent almost a third of our marriage living in the Middle East because of his job in the Navy. Twelve years ago, we were newly married and living in Bahrain. I was doing a couple of odd jobs on base, but basically I was not working. Steve, on the other hand, was working nonstop. So that meant I had time. Free, discretionary time. Like I've never had before or since.

What happened, in that spaciousness, is that I picked up a pen and I began writing. I wrote what felt like a world's worth of words that had been bottled up inside me and came tumbling out. I was lost in my own world, in all the best ways, and I awakened to an internal world that had been dormant. During that year away, words and stories broke free, spilled out of me.

I have always written. Always. Since I was a very young child. And my adult self—my newlywed, twentysomething, totally un-scheduled self— returned to writing. Returned to the soul voice.

When we are quiet, and give ourselves space, isn't it interesting what emerges? Often, I've found, we return to something familiar more than we arrive at something new. But we are returning to the familiar in a new time and a new space and in a new body, perhaps, and that gives the familiarity new signifi-cance. But it was there all along. Resting in our intuitive self. A divine expansion.

Maybe our soul voice was protecting this "deeper yes" for us, until we could return. Until we had the time or the space or the courage to return. In that way, we owe so much to her because she guards what we are unable to access until we are able.

So there I was, in the Middle East, with so few expectations of me and even fewer interruptions, and I returned to something I didn't even know I had left. Sometimes the most foreign places can be where we find our most familiar self. Crazy, right?

We had just received orders to return to San Diego, and I sat down on the floor of Flat 41 and asked God what I should do when we got back. I didn't have a job waiting for me, and besides, I had some awakenings that I didn't want to ignore, that—in fact—I wanted to honor. But I didn't know how. I didn't know what it was supposed to look like going forward. I knew I couldn't stay sequestered on the other side of the world forever, and yet I had no idea how to integrate my soul stirrings with the future that was waiting for me.

If you've ever been through any kind of reentry, which I'm pretty sure we all have in some form, you understand what it's like to have been through something significant—something that is now lodged in your soul—and to try to walk back into a world where you look pretty much the same on the outside but are completely unrecognizable on the inside.

This is a staggering chasm to navigate.

I wanted the awakening to accompany me back. And, of course, it did. But it isn't the same, is it? Not when you're back in the noise. I had an inkling of this, and so I asked God to show me how to honor what had happened to me there in the Middle East because I couldn't see how to leave it behind, but I couldn't see how I was supposed to take it with me either.

I knew, academically, God could help me out in this situation, though he was also someone I perceived to be frustratingly cryptic. I was "going through the motions" as they say, knowing I should invite God into this situation, but not really expecting much of a clear sign.

On the floor, with a candle lit, I asked for a bit of direction. And what happened was the clearest encounter with God I had ever experienced. It was so real and so personal that if I ever doubt the existence of God or his love for me, I only have to think of that experience to be re-convinced.

In a moment, God revealed to me the next step of a new future.

He literally opened a door that I could have never, in a million years, opened for myself. He invited me to walk through it, and I did. Absolutely nothing changed overnight. If anything, it has been the slowest of unfoldings. But, there in the Middle East, he gave me a chance. That one chance changed the trajectory of these last eleven years.

When something this significant happens, I am a firm believer in never forgetting. To that end, I decided to commemorate the entire journey with a tattoo. So I chose a tattoo shop, which was painted a darling shade of turquoise and had a huge bison head on the wall, which is just the kind of juxtaposition I go for.

On the day I was to get the tattoo, my tattoo artist with the solid black tattooed arms emerged from behind the curtain with a tracing paper copy of the tattoo I had emailed her a few weeks before. She wanted to go over the drawing and touch it up so it would be tattoo-ready. There was just one problem.

The image I sent her was no larger than four inches and the image she was carrying was blown up to what might as well have been a poster.

She laid the tracing paper on my inner forearm and asked me what I thought. I felt so panicked internally. I told her it wasn't going to work. The image spanned from my wrist to my elbow when I had intended to get the tattoo just on my wrist, more or less.

This was waaaaaay too big.

My tattoo artist looked at me and said, with a sort of mustered kindness, "Well, no matter what size it is, people *are* going to be able to see it."

Yeah, got it. I was trying to get a tattoo and also hide it at the same time.

I had waited five months to get in to see her and I knew my mental health could not handle leaving and reevaluating this decision and then waiting another five months to get back in with her. I knew I wanted that image and I knew the color I wanted it too. I had the perfect aqua polish on my toes—Moon River by Lechat—that I needed her to match exactly. So the whole scene was set, except that the sample was practically crawling up my entire arm.

She said she could reduce it slightly but the detail of the henna design required she not reduce the image too small or the tattoo needle wouldn't be able to create the detail. I asked her to reduce the image as much as she could. She came back with something I had not intended to get—something so much larger than I had envisioned, yet somewhat smaller than her initial attempt—and I went for it.

Nothing about getting the tattoo hurt physically. I think I was in such a state of borderline panic about it that I was numb to the pain. My memory is only of the anxiety I felt around getting it done.

Steve and Elaine were there, offering me sparkling water and trying to make me laugh. They tried to distract me from my own nerves and they both adamantly cosigned on the new size. Steve had even said before we went that I needed to get it 25 percent bigger than I wanted. Just to be a bit more audacious.

Ugghhh. That man.

The tattoo commemorates this journey: God's whisper in my ear all those years ago—in our flat overlooking the Persian Gulf—that sent my heart pounding and my fingers flying on the keyboard and started me down a path that I am still very much in awe of today.

The tattoo commemorates a Come Apart season for me and the tenderness and struggle and overwhelmed-ness that birthed me fighting for myself in new ways. And this tattoo commemorates me, showing up with my big voice, even though I get scared. Even though.

The biggest obstacle for me with this tattoo was not the fear of the pain. It definitely wasn't "comfortable," but I have been through much worse pain, for sure. Essentially, everything related to childbirth.

My biggest obstacle to getting this tattoo was what people would think.

We all have a Soul Bully that is constantly telling us how we should be doing things. This voice never takes into consideration what's actually happening in our lives, the reality of our particular circumstances. It stands far off, making blanket judgments about what it means to be "good" and what it means to be "bad." This is every bit as unhelpful as it sounds.

What's so insane about the Soul Bully is that, as Beth-with-Dreads says, "There's no grace in his system." And she's right.

I bow to the bully because his voice is loudest, yelling at me about what it takes to be accepted by and pleasing to all the right people. But it just doesn't work. The bully drowns out essential aspects of my soul, my story.

I am asking God to help me heal from this disease of needing to know that everyone approves of everything I'm doing and saying. Of not wanting to disappoint anyone. Of not wanting to displease in any way. So, maybe as much as anything, this tattoo commemorates my brave step toward letting go of what others may or may not be thinking and welcoming my own desires. This is actually deep, incisive work for me. Goes to the core. The struggle between wanting to own my voice and yet not wanting to make any waves with it. This is the work I will continue to do, and I hope that every time I look down at my arm, I will be inspired anew to be brazen.

So many of us are dying to connect with that soul voice inside us, struggling to set him or her free, desperate to celebrate—shamelessly—our unique expressions of self. We are longing for a touch from God's transcendent hand that shifts everything, absolutely everything. And we need someone to give us the permission to be true to the work of God in our lives, letting go of how others believe we might need to be doing it.

Of course I don't think you need to get a tattoo to be your true self or to celebrate God's work in your life. But, for me, this was a huge step in owning my own story, my own voice, and my own creativity.

The tattoo is designed to look like henna, inspired by the Middle East. I chose turquoise-y aqua (a perfect blend of green and blue) because it makes me blissful, a signature color. And I chose to put it on my right arm because that is my writing hand.

Here's what is very unexpected: Every time I look at it, I think, WOW, IT'S SOOOOO BIG. And then I think, WOW, IT'S SO BEAUTIFUL. I'm a little bit afraid of it, and I love it, which is maybe the intersection where more of life needs to be lived.

I think we've all had it with being muted, even if—especially if—we've been the one muting ourselves.

On those occasions when we begin to find our soul voice, begin to offer it out into the world, we must commemorate our clarity and our courage. We must memorialize the transformative work of God in our lives. We can do that any ol' way that feels meaningful to us personally—stacking our very own stones of remembrance.[1] In a journal. Up our arm. With a paintbrush. Over coffee. On a prayer. In a message in a bottle.

So that we never forget what God has done.

Reflection & Expression

If you were to get a tattoo, what would you get? See this exercise as a way to identify something that is meaningful, symbolic, and significant to you.

For Your Brazen Board

Add an image that represents your "tattoo."

21

Disobey Your Fear

People create their own questions because they are afraid to look straight. All you have to do is look straight and see the road, and when you see it, don't sit looking at it—walk.

—Ayn Rand

Last year, Steve and I needed to make a decision about where to send the twins to elementary school. Our neighborhood public school has a fabulous reputation, is one mile from our house, and is rated a 10 out of 10 in the California public schools. But I was afraid.

Afraid of the unknown, mainly. I grew up very near the neighborhood we now live in, but I did not go to that school, so I didn't have a lot of context for it. Additionally, many of my friends were putting their kids in other schools, so I was worried about what that would look like for us and for our kids socially.

In his book *Integrity*, Dr. Henry Cloud introduced a new-to-me definition of the word *integrity*: "the courage to meet the demands of reality."[1] I have held on to that idea since first reading it.

Not run. Not hide. Not snivel. Not panic. Not freeze. Not escape. But, instead, meet. Show up and be present and meet today, with whatever it holds. Integrate instead of disintegrate.

Life is full of big decisions, moments that create trajectory in a certain direction. Rarely are those decisions and that momentum and that trajectory undoable, but still, we want to make the "right" decision the first time. We want to feel at peace with where we've landed and we don't want to have to go through the pain of undoing something that we've done. Right?

So with all this being true, it's easy to get stuck. I decided to borrow some words from Scripture and turned the whole mess over to God: "I need wisdom, God, so I'm asking for some."[2] And here is the only thing I kept hearing from him: "Leeana, do not make a decision based on fear. Don't let fear be the impetus. Don't let fear be your guiding principle. Instead, what decision would you make, Leeana, if you felt perfect freedom?"

I began to think about what I would do if I felt perfect freedom. I learned a lot about who I was trying to please, my own stories I was projecting onto my kids, my assumptions and generalizations, my places of pride. This entire kindergarten decision was also uprooting the reality that I wasn't sure I could trust my own intuition, which is a disorienting discovery.

Sometimes having the courage to meet the demands of reality means we move forward, even imperfectly, and fight against the temptation to stay stuck. We fight against the wallowing. We fight against the paralysis. We decide to believe we are, in fact, reliable observers in this world. Somehow. Some way.

We get up and brush our teeth. We go for a walk. We take a vitamin. We read one psalm. Or even just one line of one psalm.

We say a simple prayer, like, "God, I need you." We get moving in one way or another. I think this is profound.

We decide that we will have the courage to meet the demands of reality. This is the kind of woman I want to be. One who is not guided by fear. One who does not react to life to appease my fear, but one who acknowledges the fear—welcomes it even— and then moves forward in spite of being afraid.

NPR's *Invisibilia* podcast series offered an episode titled "Fearless," focused on different aspects of the fear experience.[3] One of the stories was of a woman who was born with an extremely rare disorder (only four hundred people currently living in the world are known to have this same disorder) that causes calcification of the amygdala, which is the part of the brain that translates fear. So this woman does not and cannot experience fear. She is completely fearless. Neuroscientists have studied her brain for almost thirty years and have found that in the absence of fear, other parts of our brain take over. For example, logic.

When asked what she would do if a car was racing toward her, the woman said she would move out of the way. But she wouldn't register the experience as negative, painful, or trauma-tizing in any way. The podcast was trying to argue that perhaps our hypervigilance and our constant worry about danger and threatening situations for ourselves and our loved ones may be somewhat misplaced and unnecessary. Scientists on the episode even went so far as to say that our fear is often activated— through our exposure to horrific stories and events—when we don't actually need it to be activated. This may be causing life to be more painful than necessary.

The podcast also highlighted the story of a guy who was dealing with a debilitating fear of rejection after his wife left him for another man.[4] He decided to face his fear in an attempt to overcome it through a daily exercise of what he called "Rejection Therapy." Every single day he would approach a stranger with the primary purpose of getting rejected. For example, he would ask a stranger for a ride across town and back. Or he would hand out church tracts in the grocery store. Or he would ask someone if he could have a sip of their drink in a restaurant.

"No."

"No."

"NO."

Every day he would intentionally set out to get rejected in order to get over his fear of rejection. What he noticed is that people were less rejecting than he assumed they'd be, and that he did become—over time—much more confident and less afraid. In the conclusion of the interview he says, "Fear comes mostly from the stories we tell ourselves about the situation we're in or about other people, and that story becomes a reality for us. We don't need these stories as much as we think we do."

He ends with a triumphant, "I disobeyed my fear," which is such a cool line.

As the time approached for us to make a decision about Luke and Lane's school, I knew God was right. I needed to make a decision based on freedom and not fear. I needed to disobey my fear. By that time I had toured seven schools, and I needed to summon the courage to meet the demands of our reality.

What would I do if I felt total freedom?

The answer came toward me with ease: I'd choose the public school down the street from our house. And that's exactly what we did.

Fast-forward to the last month of kindergarten when I was hugging Luke and Lane's teacher a little too tight at the end-of-the-year open house and whispering "Thank you" in her ear while I cried. She hugged me back, even though I know she thought I was so creepy.

Reflection & Expression

What would I do if I weren't afraid?

If I felt perfect freedom, what would I do?

For Your Brazen Board

Find an image that portrays freedom to you.

22

Explore Dimensionally

[God has] set eternity in the human heart.

—Ecclesiastes 3:11 NIV

In ancient myth, womanhood is typically manifested in three distinct phases: maiden, mother, old woman.

The maiden is the young unbridled beauty, full of enthusiasm and promise. The mother is the embodiment of fertility, sexuality, and stability. The old woman—sometimes referred to as the beautiful crone—typically serves as a guide to the hero or heroine. She is the voice that helps the hero find his way back home, back to himself, back to greater knowledge of the world and of the divine. Sometimes blind, she is the character with all the vision and can see what others in the story never can.

When we think about who we are and who we are becoming, I believe it's helpful to think of these phases of womanhood all within our identity.

We have a young child in every one of us. That child gives us clues about passion, curiosity, play. She is the part of us that roamed and dabbled and risked without knowledge of conformity. It does not occur to this child that there is a right or wrong way to paint, a right or wrong way to climb, a right or wrong way to play. She is innocent, but she is also highly intuitive and unapologetic.

I observe the way my kids play. They are original creatives— all three of them. They do not watch what other people make. They spin ideas out of their own minds and they pile scraps and objects to make their ideas come to life. They take a laundry bag and hang it from a tree and steal salami from the fridge while I've got my back turned at the kitchen sink. They hang the net bag from a tree and cut a small hole in the corner and they tear up bits of salami and carrot and make a luring line toward their bag. "Mom, do you want to come see the lizard trap we made?"

My children are inventors, and they are unself-conscious in their craft. I watch their minds work and their hands follow, and I believe they will teach me more than I could learn from any expert. They teach me how to return, how to unlearn, how to focus intently on dabbling. They are my mentors.

And then there is the phase of womanhood I find myself in now: the mother who is learning the fine art of nurturing, care-taking—of others, yes, but of herself too. She is learning how to make peace with herself. She is learning the craft of taking exceptional care of her brood and her body. She is learning all of life's beautifully difficult lessons. Somewhere in the intensity and the longing and the dizzying days, she is listening for her soul, making sure it's still in there, giving it space as she can. She envies the freedom of her younger years, and she is grateful to be right where she is too—expanding, listening, desiring. She also longs to be settled, rooted, anchored. Not just geographically, but spiritually, emotionally, mentally, physically.

This mother knows, deep down, there is someone in her soul who is all these things already. Deep calls to deep and something within her transcends past or present or future. Wildly, momentarily, she accesses this deeply resilient, storied, wrinkled version of herself and she breathes. This is the older woman within, the voice of home, of rest, of wisdom, of prayer, of insight.

The beautiful old woman is, in Elizabeth Gilbert's words, "the old lady who lives inside me, whom I hope to someday be." She speaks the same language as my longings; she knows the persistence of them. When I explore and create and go to the garden of my soul, she nods. "Yes," she says, "this is the way."

The film *Advanced Style* has captured a handful of beauties walking the streets of Manhattan. This documentary follows women in their later years who see their sense of style as an essential manifestation of personal expression. It's a conversation about aging and beauty and creativity. And these women are amazing! A ninety-year-old with peachy orange eyelash extensions, for example. Another who says she dresses up "for the theatre of her life, every day." They are extraordinary Miss Havishams, dripping with stories and eccentricity.

I'm drawn to these women not so much for their eccentricities but for the comfort they feel in their own skin, with their own aesthetic. They are unconventional in their risks, and I'm excited by people who show us how they're living their own art instead of becoming a replica of someone else's. I believe maturity and experience, like our children, can teach us how to return—in pure forms—to uninhibited expression.

All three of these parts of us give us clues about who we are and who we are becoming: our dabbling child, our expanding mother, our self-possessed and self-expressed older woman.

Spend time with these parts of yourself. Let them speak to you. Let God speak to you through them. They will show you glimpses of eternity here on earth, of how you are to be anchored in your unshakable worth and how you are to wing your way into this world too. How you are both earth and eternity commingled.

In Hebrews, there is a passage about the heroes of our faith, those who "accepted the fact that they were transients in this world. People who live this way make it plain that they are looking for their true home. . . . You can see why God is so proud of them, and has a City waiting for them."[1]

These words make me long for the Home Country, and long for Home-Country-living here too. We long because he set eternity in our hearts, and so as we investigate what he has written there on our hearts, we are linked to past, present, future. We see, like we never have before, that we were made in an image that is three-dimensional.

Reflection & Expression

What does the child or maiden in you know?

What does the mother in you know?

What does the older woman in you know?

How is God using each of these parts of you to give you courage?

For Your Brazen Board

Find images or words that represent these phases of your life.

146

23

You Are That Girl

Apparently there is nothing that cannot happen today.

—Mark Twain

Recently, I attended an art workshop with Elaine. I like going to art workshops because they help me get my hands on my own life, help me exhale, and help me chase my intuition.

During part of the workshop we were invited to roam around the room and pick up objects to include in the art piece we were creating. Objects that spoke to us. Objects we were intuitively drawn to. Objects that told our story even if we didn't know the story yet.

Elaine saw a large peacock feather she immediately loved. She circled it a few times, even reached for it. But she didn't pick it up.

Four of us were sharing a long rectangular table, and when we all returned to the table with our supplies to begin working on our art piece, we were inspecting each other's found objects. As our hands moved, our mouths began to move, and Elaine confessed there was a gorgeous peacock feather she really wanted, but she didn't grab it.

"Why?" we all asked.

"I guess because I didn't think I deserved it," she said before she had time to edit her answer.

We all stopped what we were doing and looked up at her.

And before any of us said anything to her, Elaine said, "I should go get the feather, huh?"

"Yep," we all said in unison.

And she did. It was gorgeous and bigger than many of the other objects on the table. When I saw it, I could see why it felt presumptuous to her to take it and use it. Like perhaps it was a waste. Or, as she said, it was too special and too lovely to be deserved.

What's funny is that the feather made sense to me there on the table in front of Elaine. It was tall, like she is. Wild and beautiful, but also delicate and fragile. All like her.

I could see why she was immediately and intuitively drawn to it, and I could also see why she couldn't take it right away. It represented the "she" she hopes to be, but couldn't quite believe she already is.

I guess we can all think of a woman we know who is "that girl." The one who deserves the peacock feather and, of course, knows it. Not in a gratuitous way. Just in an I-know-who-I-am-and-what-I-like sort of way. The woman who has a clear sense of her own personal aesthetic, who is self-possessed.

So many of us know who "that girl" is and we are convinced that we are not her.

What's funny is I think of Elaine as "that girl" in so many ways. She's a stage or two ahead of me in life, and she is successful in so many ways. She has clear thoughts and opinions and knows her own voice. She trusts her instincts and she usually follows them. Which is why it was interesting to me that when it was time to pick up the peacock feather, she didn't . . . or couldn't.

What this tells me is that—likely—somewhere inside even the most centered of us all is a place where we are uncertain, adolescent, not quite sure what the rules are and how they apply to us. We perceive someone else to be holding the whistle and, if we move toward something we are assuredly not supposed to have, the whistle will be blown.

Elaine gave me permission to tell the peacock feather story to participants at an art workshop I was hosting. I said that when it was their turn to go find objects and they found something that took their breath away there on the table, I told them they very well might also hear a little voice inside their head saying, "Don't you dare pick that up. It's too much. It's too nice. It would be presumptuous to think you should use that. Pick something less dramatic. Pick something smaller. Pick something simpler. Pick something more practical. Who do you think you are?"

I told them to talk right back to that voice and say, "Who do I think I am? I am *that girl*."

Because you are . . . *you are that girl*. Even if you don't think you are. Even if your mother has spent your lifetime convincing you that you aren't. Even if you had teachers or coaches or mentors or friends or partners or church leaders or colleagues who spent time and energy trying to convince you that you would never, in the history of ever, be worthy of the peacock feather.

And I'm so sorry. I'm sorry they knocked you down. I'm sorry they assumed it was OK to come after you and damage you in those ways. I'm sorry they did violence to your soul. I'm sorry they never really saw you.

I hope you have a giant screaming tribe in your actual, real life. People who are just nuts about you and tell you all the time that you are gold. But if by chance you don't, I will stop right here and tell you what I know to be true: *You are that girl.*

At some point in life—maybe even today—you're going to metaphorically walk by a table of objects and you're going to see the most beautiful peacock feather and you're going to reach for it and then that voice inside you is going to slap your hand and say to you, "How dare you? Who do you think you are!" and you're going to recoil.

And then you're going to regret it.

Because something inside of you, something true and intuitive that was stamped on your soul the day you were created, knows what you love and knows what you want and sees such specific beauty in that peacock feather. But the voices of scarcity and shame and judgment—the Soul Bullies—were on the prowl, and wouldn't let you come alive in that moment.

And every time we let the Soul Bullies win, every time we believe we are not and will never be THAT GIRL, we give a bit of our self over to being silenced.

So I'm saying it one more time: You are that girl.

You can paint your kitchen a wild color.

You can wear that statement necklace.

You can go back to school.

You can apply for your dream job.

You can be a mother.

You can sing.

You can dance.

You can wear a bikini.

You can rock red lipstick.

You can become a runner.

You can be sensual.

You can let your hair go curly.

You can get a tattoo.

You can go back to work.

You can call yourself creative.

You can call yourself beautiful.

You can call yourself strong.

You are that girl.

Pick up the peacock feather, for crying out loud. In doing so, you are honoring the sacred space inside you that no one can get their hands on, no one can wreck. You are joining the song God already sings over you, and you are celebrating who you are becoming.

Do you know what it means to celebrate? The word literally means to "assemble to honor." The same Latin word, *celebrare*, also means to "practice often." Every time you allow yourself to expand and become, every time you allow yourself to return to the garden of your own soul, you are assembling to honor. Let's do that for ourselves and for each other. Let's assemble to honor and let's practice often. Let's join the chorus of creation, which is our worship.

Reflection & Expression

I do not deserve _____.

For Your Brazen Board

Read "Still I Rise" by Maya Angelou. Pick out a word or phrase or line from that poem.

24

Don't Walk on Your Knees

You do not have to walk on your knees for a hundred miles through the desert, repenting.

—Mary Oliver, "Wild Geese"

Apologize when you have done something wrong, when you have made a mistake. But just for the record, the following are not wrong or a mistake:

Taking up space in the world
Being alive
Using oxygen
Having a body
Asking a question
Needing a nap
Living
Dreaming

I was looking at grapefruits the other day in Vons and someone came up next to me to look at grapefruits too. I immediately apologized—"Oh, I'm sorry"—assuming that my existence was in this person's way. I do this at the airport. At the post office. At the grocery store. When I'm working in the kitchen with someone.

I apologize for my personhood.

I took a hot yoga class the other evening with Tina and Erica and it was like therapy. Part of it was the heat, the movement, the candlelight in the corners of the room, but a big part of it was our teacher. She explained to us that our theme for the evening would be truthfulness, being truthful with our bodies, our limits. Throughout our practice she encouraged us to find our highest and best selves and to be truthful about what was "highest and best" for us that night. At one point in the class, when she was reminding us about our intention of truthfulness, she said, "Just to be clear, truthfulness is not the same thing as judgment."

Man, that got me.

Truth = I take up space in the world.

Judgment = I must apologize for the space I take up in the world because it's too much, too in-the-way, and too annoying to every other space-taker-upper in this world.

Truth = I have a body.

Judgment = I must apologize for my body and its particular maladies because if I don't, everyone will think I'm just fine with my body, which is obviously not possible or acceptable.

Truth = I need to breathe.

Judgment = I must apologize for the number of breathers I personally need because I am annoying the heck out of everyone with my out-of-breathness.

An apology is an admission that you have done something wrong, so the next time you are tempted to say "I'm sorry," be sure you're saying those words because you have made a mistake or hurt someone. But whatever you do, do not utter the words "I'm sorry" because you believe you need to beg forgiveness for being alive.

You are allowed to look at grapefruits as long as you need to.

Reflection & Expression

I will no longer apologize for _____.

For Your Brazen Board

Write "I'm not sorry" somewhere.

25

Watch for Rescue

A certain darkness is needed to see the stars.

—Osho

When we lived in Bahrain, every week I would drive through an alley where the same housedresses were drying on the clothesline outside the house on the corner. Bright florals gracing an otherwise run-down neighborhood. A dark area of town, to be honest.

In fact, this neighborhood was consistently the site of burning tires and violence because of the civil rights riots we lived in and around. This particular alley was a volatile little pocket subjected night after night to tear gas and graffiti. We wouldn't go there after sunset, but every morning I drove through the alley and every morning it showed signs of the previous evening's anger and uprising.

So I loved laundry day. The festive dresses flapping in the breeze were always especially stunning. Right next to scorched concrete. Right next to angry graffiti. Pretty pinks. Bright turquoise. Greens. Browns like rich earth. One shoulder of tiny floral pinned over the shoulder of a larger scale floral, a dozen or so down the line that way. Like the prettiest store window you've ever seen.

For me, there's so much poetry in a juxtaposition. I love when worlds collide, moments overlap, and we have the everydayness of laundry happening there in the midst of heartbreak.

Sometimes life is a terrorized alley of burning tires and graffiti and fear. And then we see—against all odds—a row of humble housedresses rebelliously waving in the face of the darkness, like brazen little flags. Scenes like this speak the words our souls are longing to say:

I will not let the Hard thing bury me. I will not be hidden behind the rubble. I might be scared but I am resilient. I might be humble but I will rise against the bullies and the hooligans. I will get up and wash something.

I was recently standing on the shore of Lake Tahoe, which is drought-low, and the shoreline is pushed back over a hundred yards from where it normally starts. Ground is bare where water once was. Lots of gravelly ground. Where the water had previously been, someone had gathered medium-sized rocks, maybe a hundred of them, and fashioned a labyrinth in the middle of the exposed expanse. Kids walked single-file through the spiral, carrying their buckets and shovels, laughing. Tourists stopped to take pictures of the formation. I watched a few adults walk the coil quietly.

These metaphors—the housedresses in the midst of madness, the sacred path in the midst of drought—are eternity colliding with earth.

In 1 Samuel, God used the most humble to fell the most hooligan. He took a shepherd and he put him up against a giant, and the shepherd boy with his five smooth stones and unarmored body prevailed. Young David, holding the head of his opponent in his hands, looked at the armies who had been laughing at him moments before and said, "Everyone will know that the Lord does not need weapons to rescue his people."[1]

God rescues us with housedresses. He rescues us with smooth stones. He rescues us with paths in the wasteland. He rescues us with mica, pepper trees, bougainvillea blooms.

So the next time you feel threatened or intimidated or shamed or silenced, and the Soul Bullies are calling for your very self on a platter delivered into the hands of your plaguing enemies, you can think about these Bahraini housedresses, strung in a line, shoulder to shoulder, hanging directly above pocked asphalt and burning rubble. You can think of David, bringing a giant down with one blow. You can think of the rock path formed on barren land. Markers of hope. Reminders of victory. A nova in the darkness.

Reflection & Expression

Write about something beautiful that has emerged from something difficult.

For Your Brazen Board

Find an image of rescue or victory.

26

Curate Your Life

With an eye made quiet ... we see into the life of things.

—William Wordsworth

I have an anxious habit of collecting, but then like a frog in the pot of boiling water, all of a sudden I feel overheated by the amount of clutter around me. Every horizontal surface is covered. Every closet is packed. Every drawer is stuffed. And it's all closing in on me. Nothing feels pretty or useful or creative anymore. It all just feels like stuff. And I want to light a fire in the backyard and start over.

What is occurring to me is that I'm not only strangled by all the stuff visually but also strangled by what it represents emotionally. Usually, it's a sign of my need. I'm mindlessly piling more and more and more into our house and car and closets because I'm not taking the time to figure out what I'm really after, what's actually going on inside me.

This overindulgence or hoarding is a form of hiding, a way we cover up and cover over as a means of comfort instead of facing whatever reality we don't want to face. What is the source of my dissatisfaction? What am I trying to ease? How am I trying to make myself feel better?

When I'm refusing to tend to my actual need, I'm grabby. I grab food, clothes, accent pillows, another glass of wine . . . things I've come to believe will help me feel better because the need feels too scary, too nebulous, too tiresome. Turning toward my needs feels like too much work. My insides feel too high maintenance. So I go for "more more more," and what I end up with is "less less less."

I've started doing two things:

First, every time I start to feel anxious swirling energy about needing more or different stuff, I ask God to help me channel that same energy into taking exceptional care of my body instead—namely, exercising and eating nourishing food and drinking water. Every time I start to feel panicky about more, more, more, I realize that taking care of my body will help me feel so much better—in the long run—than more food, more clothes, more stuff.

I *love* beautiful things. I *love* rich experience and luscious meals. I *love* surrounding myself with interesting textures and creative details and layers of color. This is a part of my soul that does not need denying. Wanting to create an interesting home or wear unique pieces of clothing does not equal mindless hoarding. But you know as well as I do when we're looking to these things to fix us, when we're *using*. You know as well as I do when we're grabbing because we're trying to solve a problem that food, clothes, pillows never will.

So my attempt to take care of my body is a way I can use my anxious energy to my own benefit. I can teach myself how to nurture my body instead of numb it.

Second, I've been challenging myself to do the refining work of deciding what I love and only bringing those things into my home and closet.

Will it bring me pleasure?

Will I reach for it over and over again?

Will it speak to me?

Or is it just one more thing, one more quick fix?

And, on top of that, I'm starting to ruthlessly get rid of the things in my house I don't love. A long time ago I read an article about a woman who got rid of every single thing in her house that she didn't like aesthetically, all the way down to pens and sticky notes. If it wasn't pleasing to her, she didn't have it or bring it into her home. There's a part of this that feels like a luxury, but there's also a part of this I totally get. Many of us live in a sea of things that cause chaotic, overstimulating, and depressing vibes in our homes, and we assume we can't really do anything about it.

I'm very much in the beginning stages of this, but I see how our homes and our closets and our refrigerators can be these Ground Zero places where we can decide to nourish the True Self and starve out the False Self if we will approach them with intention. What a concept.

Curating has become a sort of buzzword these days, especially as minimalism seems to be making its way back into trending conversations. While I'm not a minimalist by nature, one of the things I love most about this idea of curating a selective environment is the idea that we must practice the discipline of learning what we love.

As I curate instead of amass, as I nourish instead of numb, I become more awake to the dynamics at play in my own soul. I am more attuned to my need, which is the good news and the bad news, I guess. But I am giving myself a fair shot at really, truly meeting my need instead of shoving one more quick fix down my throat.

I'm learning the fine art of selecting the elements in my spaces and my world in a way that serves my soul and my emotional sobriety. Keeps me clean instead of cluttered. I'm learning to take care of my body instead of seeing how quickly I can buy more clothes for my body. I'm learning what it means to pursue quality over quantity, to become very familiar with what I need, what I love, and the freedom that comes from narrowing. And it's really, really hard.

Anyone can amass. Not everyone can curate.

I love Myquillyn Smith's Instagram hashtag: #HushThe House. She's helped me think, very practically, about quieting my home and my closet so that I can actually *enjoy* what I have instead of needing to constantly *manage* what I have.

She tells you to take everything you can out of a room and then start adding things back in, one at a time, until the space feels nurturing but not cluttered. What you find when you do this is that you were living with far more chaos than you realized, far more visual stimulation than you intended, even. And clearing it out is like breathing again.[1]

There are many different aspects to this conversation: practical functionality, emotional underpinnings, our tendencies and preferences, the role aesthetics play in our lives and homes. But here are my conclusions: Sometimes I assume I need more when, in reality, I need less. Cutting away the excess can reveal the essential in this amazing sort of way. What we loved and needed had been there all along but we just couldn't see it through all the noise. Sometimes we perpetuate all the noise because we want a nice distraction from our need. Hushing the house and quieting the closet, then, are ways we turn down all the external ruckus so we can listen to the conversations that are happening in our hearts and souls under the surface.

I'm proud of myself for leaning into these areas of my life. They're muddy and murky and multilayered, to be sure. Anytime we're talking about the things we grab to make ourselves feel better, I'm raising my hand and saying, "Yes, I do that. Me too" and "I so wish I were beyond all that."

How about you? I'd love to know how you're making your home a haven, your closet a curated collection, and how you're doing all this as a manifestation of your Created Center. I'd love to hear how you're practicing self-possession by exercising self-restraint. And most of all, I'd love to know what your life and soul now have capacity for because you've exercised the spiritual discipline of hushing so you can really hear.

Reflection & Expression

Make a list of what you love in your closet and your home, things you already own.

Choose five items in your closet and five items in your home. Write down why you love them.

For Your Brazen Board

Add images or words that represent things you love.

Part Three

Recover

{YOUR SOUL}

27

Lock the ~~Shed~~ Studio

Take full responsibility for yourself—for the time you take up and the space you occupy.

—Maya Angelou

Two years ago I had a semi-manic episode related to a horrible brown shed.

When we bought our house, a dilapidated wooden lean-to butted out from the back of our garage. Since the day we moved in, I have felt a certain compulsion to tear down that shed and rebuild something in its place that could serve as a studio for me, a room of one's own as Virginia Woolf says.

This compulsion reached fever pitch when all of a sudden I knew that if I could just get that shed torn down and a simple little space built in its place, then my mental health would be magically restored and life's intensity would immediately dissipate.

I'm not sure if you've ever attached your happiness, much less your sanity, to something getting demoed or built or remodeled, but if you have, then you know how these things grow in intensity. The countertops become our key to joy. The nasty carpet is the one thing standing in the way of a deeply fulfilling life. And so on.

What became clear is that I needed to let it all go. I needed to stop banking my emotional equilibrium on whether or not this shed was going to be transformed. You know how it goes: money, time, priorities, la, la, la.

So I did. I let it go. But here's the kicker: two years later it finally happened! We took down the infested appendage and rebuilt a little space in its place. The new shed is part storage and part my space, but I'm hoping—help me, Marie Kondo—to pare down some of what we're storing in there so I can claim as many square inches of this new space as possible.

After the shed was finished, I fell into a euphoric trance, walking some of my very favorite and most-inspirational things down from the house to the new space. At the moment, it's highly unglamorous, but it's gonna be fabulous. I can just feel it.

I told Beth-with-Dreads about the shed-turned-studio, and do you know the first thing she asked me?

"Does it have a lock?"

Isn't that perfect? *Does it have a lock.* (I laughed out loud.)

"Yes, in fact, it does," I told her.

"Good," she said. "It's good for your kids to know that it's Mommy's space."

I'm learning to become the gatekeeper of my own soul. I get to decide who comes in and out and when and with what frequency. I get to close the door sometimes, even lock it, and keep the darlings and their precious overstimulation at bay, even for twenty minutes.

And I've begun spending time in the space. A little here. A little there. I have galvanized buckets with paints and brushes. Pieces of wood. Empty frames.

One time I went down to the shed, and right when I sat down for a moment of deep spiritual introspection, the neighbor turned on his leaf blower. And, wouldn't you know, I couldn't hear my soul over the noise. So I went back up to the house. Another time I went down to the shed with the best intentions to get lost in a painting project, and it was not one degree cooler than 115 degrees, and I had to go back up to the house for fear of heatstroke. Sometimes I go in there and flies attack me or I have to pee. If I open the door to the shed for some fresh air, I see the gorgeous olive tree that's parked right outside—but I also see electric blue foam littering the yard from the disintegrating bumpers on the kids' trampoline.

In other words, nothing about this is perfect.

Oh well.

I am more and more convinced that catching up with our intuitive, creative self is one of the most essential things we can do. Whether your creative expression is painting or cooking or gardening or tinkering with car engines or making jewelry, letting her speak to you will change you, energize you, and the inspiration will spill into other areas of your life as well.

Two years ago we moved home from the Middle East. As is the case with moves, a few things were shoved into the back of the garage and haven't been opened since. One of those things was an aqua cabinet, called a coffin cabinet—I was told by the dealer who sold it to me—because it is shaped like coffins of old. I got it at a vintage shop years ago and I bought it because

I loved the color and because we were getting ready to move overseas and I was making purchases to soothe my anxiety.

These past two years, the cabinet was sitting in the back of our garage, still sealed from the move. Steve and I carried it to the shed, and I tore off the plastic wrap and cardboard. I opened the cabinet and pulled out all the packing paper to begin loading in treasures, and I found something that took my breath away:

Inside the cabinet, underneath all the packing paper, was a dried bougainvillea bloom that had been waiting for me these two years. Waiting for me to find it at just the right time. Bougainvillea is like a divine wink to me. Some people find hearts in nature or lucky pennies. I find bougainvillea petals and it's like God is saying to me, "I see you and you're on the right track and keep listening and keep creating and I love you." One bougainvillea bloom says all that to me. And this one, transported all the way from the Middle East, said all that and more. It was an affirmation and a confirmation and in some kind of weirdly perfect way, a complete and total YES to following my brazen heart.

Everywhere I go these days, I see the bright blooms of bougainvillea. It's everywhere here in Southern California, of course, but what I keep seeing—what keeps speaking to me— are the paper-like petals that have left the vine and are scattered here and there. They seem to blow off the vines easily in our breezes, and so they're strewn all over the ground.

A few flashes of hot pink at my feet on a neighborhood run or in the tall wheat-colored grasses around my house are like nature's confetti.

I read somewhere that bougainvillea symbolizes protection. I can see that. Not only is it beautiful but it also has sharp spines that can poke you if you're not paying attention. And it also vines in a way that creates thick "hedges of protection." Somewhere else I read that bougainvillea symbolizes passion, which also works for me.

I'll go with both: protection and passion. Seems like just about everything a girl could want in life.

In my twenty minutes of soul time, I ask God if there's anything he wants to tell me. Over and over again, he says, "Follow your inner artist. Honor your inner artist. Listen to your inner artist. Welcome your inner artist."

It's certainly not a far stretch to consider that all these things—the shed, the twenty minutes of soul time, the inner artist, the bougainvillea—are all connected. The meaning of the bougainvillea puts perfect words to it for me: protection and passion. I am longing for a harbor for my soul and also, in the safety of that place, an opportunity for expression.

It seems so fitting to think about the feminine image of God sitting with me in this space—both a guide toward my greatest passions and a wise protector too, showing me how to honor my soul by being a gatekeeper.

Beth-with-Dreads encourages me to allow this space to also be a place of nonproductive creating, the kind of work we do that is simply for pleasure. Some of us are so disconnected to what brings us pleasure. It's felt taboo to even consider what's pleasing to us, especially if it's not practically productive.

I certainly take my laptop down to the shed, but not always. The shed is a place of sacred offering, of worship, where I protect my soul so I can pour out passion. It's an unfinished little rectangle—nothing much in light of the whole world—a place to play, to get lost in a world of my own making.

Steve had the kids in the hot tub while I poked around in the new space. Before I joined them, I cut a long, flowering tendril off a potted bougainvillea near our front door. I put the stem in the white hobnail vase that was my grandmother's and then my mother's and I put the simple arrangement in the center of the table I set up in the studio.

I closed and locked the door and went off to find my family.

Reflection & Expression

If you were creating your own space, what would you put in it?

For Your Brazen Board

Add images of the elements you listed above.

28

Risk like Rowan and Rousey

> Growth demands a temporary surrender of security.
>
> —Gail Sheehy

Every Midshipman at the Naval Academy is assigned the essay "A Message to Garcia," for required reading.[1] In the story, a fictitious young lieutenant is tasked with finding the Cuban rebel leader Calixto Garcia and getting him a vital and timely message from President McKinley. The US is embroiled in a conflict with Spain, which—according to this telling—is in control of Cuba, and McKinley would like to procure a strategic ally in the form of Garcia. Lieutenant Rowan is only given the directive of getting this message to Garcia, and it is up to him to figure out how he is going to get himself and the message to the target.

The entire essay is a lesson in initiative designed to teach each Midshipman the importance of receiving guidance and

171

then making that guidance happen even if they're not given a road map to complete the task.

Lieutenant Rowan was told to get a message to Garcia. Where was Garcia? Who was Garcia? Where was Rowan supposed to sleep once he found Garcia? Who would accompany him on his search for Garcia? How long would he be gone? What should he take in his pack? What was the proper outfit for meeting with a Cuban rebel leader? Should he take cigars and whiskey to win over Garcia? Doesn't anyone know Rowan's just a lowly lieutenant?

"A Message to Garcia" is a powerful narrative about taking a risk even if you haven't been given every single nuanced step along the way. It's about getting guidance and going for it, not letting fear of the unknown prevail, even if every last detail hasn't been spelled out. In other words, it's about taking the next right step instead of letting the entire enterprise paralyze us.

There's no real road map for growing into our soul. No formula for self-possession, expansion, investigating our desires, connecting with our longings. If anything, these are trial-and-error propositions, attempts, and revisions. We listen, we lean in, and often we learn, all the while believing there are gifts in the process, something we will take with us that we couldn't have acquired any other way.

Still, though, it's hard. To have to strain to hear God's voice and then to wonder if it was really him we heard after all. To wrestle with the tides of longing and the rushes of desire and the cycle of hope and disappointment. It's hard to wonder when we are to stop, dead still, and wait . . . and when we are to act, hard and fast, on the whispers.

What does soul initiative look like? How are we supposed to know we're on the right track?

These words from Tama Kieves, I believe, are about as helpful as anything: "Transformation of any kind always exacts a holy tussle."[2]

We know we're on the right track when we experience the holy tussle. This is counterintuitive because tussles, by nature, are uncomfortable, trying. They wear us out, and the Soul Bullies begin telling us we're not supposed to be worn out, we're not supposed to be scrimmaging for our souls. Life is supposed to arrive on the wings of ease. And if it's not? Then we better abandon our path because we're clearly misguided.

The tussle, while uncomfortable, is an indication we're on to something, I believe. It's a wink from the universe telling us we are headed in the right direction. The fairy godmothers, who are conspiring along with us, are clapping their hands. The tussle builds our muscles and tests our breath. It calls on our will, desires, secret dreams. The tussle is a sign we're engaged, which—I believe—is as important as anything.

Recently I watched Ronda Rousey fight Bethe Correia in the UFC mixed martial arts event. I'm not a huge fan of women's fighting, but I wanted to watch the fight because there had been a lot of buildup and because I like the fact that Rousey is an Olympic medalist in judo and not just a hot-mouthed brawler. A group of us watched the fight, all thirty-four seconds of it. We watched Rousey knock out her opponent in record time. But you could see how the ring is risky. Anything can happen. Rousey won decisively, but she took a shot right in the nose before she finished the fight, and that shot could have downed her. In the end, Rousey dominated Correia, but in those thirty-four seconds, you saw how anything could have happened. When we step in the ring, or in "the arena," as Theodore Roosevelt called it, we are accepting potential disappointment. We are engaging in a tussle.

Showing up with our crazy longings and our beating hearts and our sweating palms and our wide eyes . . . this is all a risk. We're likely going to take a few shots. The Brazen Warrior knows this is all normal, even necessary, to living a life that isn't dictated by shame. But that doesn't mean it's easy.

Some of us feel like we've been in the ring with God, maybe even feel like we've been knocked out, sucker punched. Wrestling with God doesn't always feel like a fair fight.

Makes me think of Jacob in the Bible, who wrestled through the night with a divine messenger, whose hip was dislocated, and who walked with a limp for the rest of his life because of the encounter. Makes me think of how, when our humanity is touched by divinity, we sometimes cringe with discomfort. But it always changes us.

We are led right into the ring and we are in the midst of such darkness. And in the struggle, we find, all of a sudden, that we have expanded in new ways, we have courage we didn't once have. The courage came to us by way of the ring. The courage was hard-won. That's why the whole thing is holy, I guess. New life doesn't get served to us on silver. Usually we have to fight for it. Birth is beautiful, but did you ever notice, painful?

At one point in my twenty minutes of soul time, God asked me this question directly: "What if you spent a little less time with your kids?"

And I burst into tears.

The tears fell out of my eyes in a way that felt like breathing. What I heard in that moment was, "What if you didn't have to carry the kind of over-responsibility you're feeling right now? What if you released them just a little bit?"

The bullies had pressed their bony fingers on my soul right where I am most vulnerable. They told me to take long gulps of shame, convincing me that I was always facing a deficit as a mother, a deficit I needed to somehow mitigate. In other words, I was behind. And no matter how my life actually looked, how my kids were actually doing, I needed to outrun my perceived failures.

If you've ever dealt with these kinds of menacing messages rattling around in your mind, then you know how they are such impossible burdens, how they exhaust you from their sheer weight and intensity. They rob you of your real life.

We tussled. What did that mean, "spend less time"? What was I supposed to do with that time? Wasn't that *cheating*? Frivolous? Shirking, at the very least? And God brought me back to the Brazen Promise and his desire for me to live lighter. I bring him my heavy (hypervigilance, over-responsibility, bought-into lies) and he gives me his light (peace, rest, truth).

Could I give myself the permission to surrender my children a bit? Could I let God take the load I was carrying? Could I trust that I am someone who can be happy and that my kids are doing great? I sensed God was saying, "It's time. It's time for you to experience freedom from this."

He showed me—in tiny, moment-by-moment ways (breathe, Leeana, breathe) and then in larger life-rhythm ways (secure more child care, Leeana)—how I was to live more surrendered. He showed me how shame can never be satisfied; we cannot do enough to fill its cavern. I cannot spend enough time with my kids to prove shame wrong. He showed me how anxiety had tried to blow out the candle in my soul, and it was time to light it again. It was time.

Time to listen to my desires. Time to let go incrementally. Time to walk, willingly, into the holy tussle. Time to get into the ring and participate. Time to face down the boney finger poking a hole in my chest. Time to let God love me in these super scary ways. Time to relight the flame in my soul.

A road map does not exist, dear friends. But I can tell you about a risk that has been mysteriously transformational:

Return. Tussle. Emerge.

Return. Tussle. Emerge.

Return. Tussle. Emerge.

Risk and reward are bedfellows, and I'm grateful that God injects us with doses of unexplainable courage even when we can't see the end from the beginning. If. We. Will. Return.

Reflection & Expression

Read Theodore Roosevelt's "The Man in the Arena" and reflect on a risk you are currently considering.[3]

Write about the holy tussle of transformation you are experiencing.

Consider:

What feels uncomfortable?

What feels exciting?

What feels vulnerable?

What feels risky?

What is ill-fitting?

Where is there light?

Where is there darkness?

Where is there struggle?

For Your Brazen Board

Add the phrase "holy tussle" somewhere or include an image that depicts your holy tussle.

29

Drop the Drapes

What's past is prologue.

—William Shakespeare,
The Tempest

I recently came across an old journal. You know how intriguing that can be, to look back at your thoughts from years ago. Especially because it's easy to move on, to forget, to disconnect from who we were back then. Or, at least, it is for me.

The entry is a letter written from me, to me.

The letter is marked October 8, 2008. On that day, I was thirty-two years old. I was not yet a mother. I was significantly pregnant with two babies who would be born nine weeks later.

I wrote the letter to myself in ten years, which meant the thirty-two-year-old Leeana was sending her deepest thoughts on the wind to the forty-two-year-old Leeana.

I was on the precipice of life change, though I had no idea how to even anticipate, let alone prepare for, what was about to happen. Additionally, I was very much in the awful middle of my first book, which despite rewrites upon rewrites, would not come together for me. I was slightly paralyzed with anxiety, not quite sure how to reconcile who I was and who I was becoming.

The letter is dear and sentimental and I'm so grateful to have come across it. It's amazing to see what I wrote to myself about the babies, not sure what they'd look like, what their names would be.

What's most intriguing to me about this letter is the way it ends. The final paragraph reads: "I have inklings of you—parts of you I feel like I know and parts I'm sure I will discover." And then the very last line: *I hope you have felt the freedom to become.*

This is truly unreal, because I found this journal while I'm in the middle of writing a book about being brazen, about becoming, about growing into our voices and living into our longings.

It's the very thing I want for my children: that they will feel the freedom and support to become who they are meant to become, who they were created to be in their center. It's what I've always wanted for myself—one of my deepest and most enduring longings—probably because I have become in so many essential ways, but my becoming has also been thwarted in certain seasons. By anxiety. By my desire to be easily liked more than wildly loved. By my insecurities. By my intoxication with image instead of my quiet nurturing of identity.

I was writing that letter to the forty-two-year-old Leeana. I'm not there quite yet, but I am closer to her than I am to the thirty-two-year-old Leeana who wrote the letter, and I can say definitively that I'm ready to live into—as intentionally as I possibly can—the freedom to become.

I want that for you too. I see too many of us becoming more and more invisible because it suits those around us or because we're afraid of what standing up and standing out might cost us. We are afraid to become and live from our beautiful and bold Created Center.

Or, as Ann Kidd Taylor put it, "I learned how easy it is to give up and become draperies while everyone else is dancing."[1]

Doesn't that just nail it?!

Perhaps becoming draperies has served us. It's what we've chosen for ourselves. It's what other people in our lives have expected us to be. Or becoming draperies was how we kept everyone happy. But somewhere along the way we got lost. We got lost behind depression or our empty nest or our abuse or our need to be perceived as nice or even our piles of laundry. We got lost behind responsibility or fatigue or misunderstanding. We got lost behind fear or our inability to fight for ourselves. We got lost behind the weight of our responsibilities.

Are we ready for a new way? Are we ready to consider what it might be like to drop the drapes and get on the dance floor? Are we ready to become?

Become is a great word. Its etymology is "to come to a place, come to be or do something, receive." The definition is "to begin to be, to undergo change or development." It's kind of a contradiction within itself to both "be" and "come"—a state and an action all in the same word. I like to think of becoming as both waiting and receiving, which is really the essence of the dance.

We are both onward and waiting. We are both being and coming. We are both pursuing and receiving. We are holding the tension of a state of being and an action at the same time. In this tension is where we learn the dance. We learn the movements of returning—to God, to the whispers and nudges of our Created Center, to the garden of our own soul where we are given freedom to roam. In this way, the movement is back to something inexplicably familiar, like home, and yet mysteriously unexplored.

The dance, then, is not some boisterously obnoxious display. It's not about attention seeking. The dance is about allowing God to show us around what he already knows, who we already are, and—like the hummingbird who migrates thousands of miles and then returns to the same garden on the same day, year after year—our home.

As we drop the drapes and step into the dance, we get glimpses of our Created Center that God is inviting us to investigate. And, somewhere down deep, we know that true freedom is not chasing after the forbidden but, instead, embracing the already.

I want to make good on what that thirty-two-year-old me wrote to the forty-two-year-old me. I want to honor her by showing her that, yes, in fact, I am becoming. Slowly and surely, I am becoming.

I'm unwilling to let my Created Center be muted. And so I begin again. I return to the Creator, the ultimate artist. Some days the dance steps feel awkward and unpracticed. And then there are the days when I realize I'm learning a rhythm I always, already knew.

Reflection & Expression

Write a letter to who you will be in ten years. What do you want to say to that older version of yourself?

In what ways are you drapery?

What does dancing represent to you?

For Your Brazen Board

Add a picture of someone dancing.

30

Paint Nightlights

Art enables us to find ourselves and lose ourselves at the same time.

—Thomas Merton

I didn't sleep well as a child. I worried about the sounds I heard, people coming into our house. Additionally, my mind was always going. That is still true today. Now, sleep is one of the few times I feel peaceful. My mind reels when I'm awake. I don't know how other people's minds work but I often wonder if they're as busy and restless as my own. Some of this is good—ideas, thoughts, connections. Some of it is debilitating.

As a child I carried these sensitivities and I think they kept me up at night—wondering and wandering, and sometimes worrying. At night, while I was waiting for sleep, I would take out the nontoxic nail polish I got in a makeup kit for Christmas, and I would paint the nightlight that was plugged into a socket on the south wall of my bedroom. I would paint it and then wait for the heat from the bulb to dry the polish and then I'd peel it off in long strips like you peel a fruit roll from the plastic wrapper.

Then I'd paint it again. Wait for it to dry and peel. Paint and peel. Paint and peel. Until sleep arrived.

Those trained in Somatic Experiencing would probably tell you I was using the nightlight as an anchor, a way to orient all of the disorientation, a focal point. In the past, I've thought of this as sort of an example of my just being a super weird kid. Now I'm beginning to believe my late-night art exploits might have more to tell me.

Recently I realized I felt a bit of envy when I remembered myself and the nightlight.

What are you envious of? I wondered.

And the following came to mind: *She is lost in her own world.*

The nightlight-painting child inside me is lost in a world of her own making, creating something that interests her. There is no audience, no one to please. There is no TRY. She is simply delighted by the world she's entered.

Within a few years of this story, I would be worried about belonging, where I fit in. I would worry about whom, exactly, I would sit with at lunch and who, exactly, my friends were. The prospect of appearing as though I didn't have a tribe, a place, was troubling to me. At some point I would begin to feel like I was composed entirely of one million raw nerve endings.

But before all that was the six-year-old me in my bedroom, late at night, and I think she's probably an important version of me to reconnect with, lost in her own magical world.

These days, I long for the time and space to get lost. Getting lost in my own world doesn't always seem compatible with my current life responsibilities. But that doesn't mean I give up. I just have to get creative. Luckily, I'm good at that. How can I become that little girl again, painting the nightlight, lost in a quiet world of my own making? How can I find my way back to her pure intuition?

The times in my life when I have been the most unhappy are the times when I've neglected that little girl and her longing to get lost in a creative world. She wasn't looking for approval or applause. This was about something much more essential and true.

As a thirty-nine-year-old homeowner and mother of three, this feels frivolous, like I don't have this kind of time to waste. Life feels significantly more urgent. But my feelings of over-responsibility are what begin to drown me. Yes, I'm responsible for my home. Yes, I'm responsible for my kids. Yes, I'm responsible for a whole host of things, but when those responsibilities become so heavy that I am unable to live freely and lightly anymore, when everything other than my responsibilities begins to feel frivolous and engaging in creativity is nothing but self-indulgent . . . something is off.

My hypervigilance is actually keeping me from connection to others and my life in meaningful ways. Isn't that interesting? We feel over-responsible for everyone else and under-responsible for ourselves.

I've come to realize that the best way I can live, the way I so deeply long to live, is both lost in my own worlds and deeply connected. I am actually yearning—in all the best ways—for these things.

Currently, I'm letting my intuition off the leash a bit. I'm letting her run free with the intention of leading me toward worlds I'm longing for and neglecting. I'm talking back to that voice inside that keeps telling me how ridiculous my soul voice is and how much important time she's wasting. I'm talking back to that Soul Bully who wants to strangle me with expectations and hypervigilance and over-responsibility. It's no way to live.

Walking around the grounds of a gorgeous park when I'm on a tight deadline might seem like a terrible waste of time. But I'm seeing how the beauty and the creativity spark me and I actually have more energy to work and be and live when I have gone into these worlds that speak to me. I'm charging my own batteries. I'm allowing myself to be healed and inspired and spoken to. I'm getting quiet and seeing what surfaces. It's pretty cool.

I think that's why the six-year-old me keeps coming to my mind. She's the unlikely midwife, helping bring dabbling and delight back into my world.

Reflection & Expression

What did you love to do as a child? How did you play?

For Your Brazen Board

Include an image of a child that speaks to you.

31

Pick Pomegranates

What if you wake up some day, and you're 65 ... and you were just so strung out on perfectionism and people-pleasing that you forgot to have a big juicy creative life?

—Anne Lamott

When I was a kid, my brother Trey and I used to climb the neighbors' fence and pick pomegranates from their tree. My mom would let us eat the pomegranates as long as we put our bathing suits on and got in the bathtub to eat them. That way she could contain the dark, delicious juice.

Steve and I bought a house about—as the crow flies—a mile or so away from my childhood home. On one of the routes back to our house, I drive by a spindly pomegranate tree in the front yard of someone we don't know. At a certain time of year, the tree has red-wine ornaments dangling from its branches that seem far too spindly to hold such luscious fruit.

I slow the car way down in front of the house—like a total creeper. I take a picture of it and post it to Instagram.

"What are you *doing*, Mom?" the kids groan and moan from the backseat.

I tell them about me, the pomegranates, and the tub. And how their Uncle Trey and I would sit in the tub and smear the magenta juice all over the sides of the tub and ourselves. We'd pucker our mouths if the seeds were too tart. And at some point the inside of our mouths would start to shrivel from all the acid.

My kids laugh at this. I find I'm salivating.

"Then Gran would come in and spray us down, and I'd watch the pink water swirl toward the drain."

"Can we go home already?" someone chimes in.

"Sure," I say.

And I put the car back in drive and start heading down the hill and then up the hill toward our house.

The thing is—and I don't think my kids have caught on to this yet—that tree is on the stretch of road on the "long way" home. It's not the most efficient route into and out of our neighborhood. But I'm learning to listen to that voice inside me that's asking for doses of beauty, even if those hits are only found on the long way home, even if I have to drive out of my way to breathe.

I believe God created the world as a playground of inspiration to us. And the beauty we find in it is unique to each person here, like an individual poem or song he has written to you and to me, and he's hidden the words and the stanzas and the melodies and the verses in the nooks and crannies of the world and has set us free to find those things that speak to us uniquely. His very word, spoken to you, spoken to me, is lurking around us.

For some of you, it's elephants. You love elephants. And you get weepy looking at elephants because their big ears and their long eyelashes are so friendly and elegant, and when you see an elephant at the zoo or a picture of an elephant, you just feel like the world is a better place. That elephant inspires you.

Maybe for you, you can breathe when you have a collection of extra-fine-tip Sharpie markers in your bag. And when you look into your bag and you see hot pink and lime and turquoise and chocolate brown caps, you smile and you feel like the universe is speaking to you, beckoning you, through those markers.

For some of you, it's the sky. And it whispers to you as it changes all day long. And if you take the time in your day to actually listen to what it wants to say to you, you find yourself absolutely hypnotized and really breathing.

Maybe one of your primary inspirations is music. Music is, for you, a teleporter or a time machine or a cocoon or a life raft. And when the right music is on, you are transported and enveloped and saved. And your soul feels as if it has been cut open in all the best ways.

Maybe some of you find great inspiration in other people's creativity. And though you may not be able to come up with ideas or projects or recipes on your own, you love looking at what other people have created and that breathes ideas and life into you, and it motivates you (inspires you!) to get up off the couch and do a little something. So you need to find time to look at other people's creativity—books, blogs, HGTV, and so on.

Maybe you need to get your body moving. And when you do, you find that your brain kicks into this other gear and, though it's so hard to find the time to do it, getting your heart rate up and your body moving and your skin sweating brings you back to life.

Maybe you like going to salvage yards and garage sales and junk stores and digging through discarded items to find something strange and wonderful that you might refashion into this interesting piece of original artwork. And when you do that, you feel like you have just come alive for the first time and again.

Perhaps this is a week when you might go in search of an elephant, purchase some Sharpies, spend some intentional time with the sky, put on your headphones, visit a museum, take a walk, troll some garage sales Saturday morning.

Like our cars, our lives do not work when we're on E. Sure we can run on fumes for a time, but at some point we must go about filling up.

I believe it's worth your time to engage your senses even if that engagement requires some inefficiencies. This is one of the ways we reacquaint ourselves with ourselves. We remember what we love, what tastes good, what looks beautiful. We remember what we enjoyed as children, how we played, how our fingers looked stained with pomegranate juice. We remember we were made for the garden in all its abundance.

Some might consider the beauty-chase a waste. Engaging your senses might take time, energy, gas, paints, paper, firewood, a babysitter.

One of the dictionary definitions of the word *waste* is "wild area." Were we taught to bow down to efficiency, conservation at all costs, and stewardship in ways that have now frightened us away from slow and present experience? Are we honoring practicality above all? Has the "wild area" become too much? Have we made time for the taste-and-see of life?

These are all things I think about as I'm winding my way through town or working in my house or walking outside. I catch a glimpse of something otherworldly—through the window or on the wind—and my soul perks up like it recognizes the howl.

I want to honor this call.

The kids and I pull into our driveway and start unpacking the inexplicable amount of flotsam and jetsam that makes its way in and out of our minivan every day. As we're unloading, Lane asks, "Hey, Mom, can we eat a pomegranate in the tub sometime?"

"Yes, dolly," I say. "Let's do that."

Reflection & Expression

What inspires you?

For Your Brazen Board

Find an image of something that inspires you.

32

Unlearn

The most useful piece of learning for the uses of life is to unlearn what is untrue.

—Antisthenes

A few months ago, Steve returned from a hunting trip with this glimmering peace in his eyes, as if he had just seen the other side of things and had come back to tell me how beautiful it is in paradise. He had only gone to New Mexico, but New Mexico looked good on him. He told me how he spent hours just walking through the desert, alone, in silence.

"What was so good about that?" I ask.

"Being out there is all about unlearning," he says.

Recently I attended an art workshop called the "Story Box Workshop." Our facilitator led us in a guided meditation that informed the direction of our story boxes. In my meditation, I saw Luke and Lane on the swings in our backyard. That was the clear image God gave me. I think, in part, because every time I think of Luke and Lane, deep, primal feelings are conjured. Feelings about them, for sure. But maybe even more so, feelings about myself. And God keeps inviting me back to that space.

Reluctantly, fearfully, scalded, I go. To his classroom of holy unlearning. Ridding my soul of all the things I've picked up and put on but are not serving me.

I wandered around the room, scanning all the tiny found objects and the compelling images and the scraps of metal and bits of anything and everything you could possibly imagine.

I kept feeling drawn toward pictures of women who were underwater: mermaids and even a woman who looked like she had fallen back into the water and was motionless. I grabbed the mermaid and the motionless woman too, even though the motionless woman scared me.

Then I found an image of a woman who had fluorescent green eye shadow and bold hot pink lips and a crazy yarn hat that was twirling and swirling around her face. She was dancing, or at least she had some kind of movement in her. Across the page was a reflection of this same woman. You could see her face and her hat but it was just a whisper of an image of her. It wasn't the saturated, wild colors of the true image. It was muted.

As I worked on my box with paint and metal and these images, I was drawn to a package of gold wire. When I snipped the small piece holding the wire in its perfect circular coil, the entire roll of it just sprung up and out and into the most impossible tangle. I sat for some time trying to work the gold wire free from itself so I could cut a piece long enough to wrap around my box the way I had it pictured in my mind.

All of a sudden the tangle resonated with me, and I stopped trying to work it out, work it out, work it out, and I just hot glued the entire tangle to the front of my box. It was the most honest thing I could say, and it looked really beautiful, actually.

I'm working with and wrestling with that tangle, I realize. The tangle of who I see when I see myself.

I wonder if grace is actually in the reduction of things, a gentle or not-so-gentle returning to the bottom line. Who we are. Who God is. How we are loved. An uncovered nakedness. Grace is the reminder that the Creator and his creation are enough: our Created Center is gold.

At first, I thought my story box would be about Luke and Lane and motherhood. As I let the process unfold, let go, and just let it happen, I realized that what I was really working on and working through was the holy unlearning of releasing the muted, distorted reflections I carry around of myself and accepting the real, saturated deal.

Bound up in the tangle are some accusations, some mantras, some fear, some deep belief. A tangle of the best ideals and the worst lies. I wrote the word *brazen* on a torn scrap and clipped it into the tangle. Because, no matter what else, I want to live from a place truer than shame.

I looked my box over and I thought of that line Steve said: "It's all about unlearning." Your Created Center exists—beautifully, organically, wildly exists. God gave you a name and a place in this world and he is calling you back to his love each and every day. He is inviting us to unlearn the muted versions of ourselves that we put out into the world and to return to his fully saturated love, our fully saturated selves.

We know he stamped beauty on our souls, and we don't know it. We believe in it and long for it, and we let it get bullied and buried too.

Maybe heaven is an eternal unlearning, a time and space of being reunited with the truth—about ourselves, about God, and about each other. A truth we have always known, intuitively, but have let ourselves forget, or even reject.

Maybe heaven-on-earth is believing that what God has already given us is enough, and that he longs to show us the breadth and depth and height and width of this already.

Unapologetically. I don't want an image, a version, or a reflection of myself. I don't want the spun stories, the faded façade. I want to be reunited with the fully saturated truth that has always been true.

Reflection & Expression

I need to unlearn _____.

For Your Brazen Board

Find an image of a person that feels like a fully saturated You.

33

Develop a Practice

If we live by the Spirit, let us also keep in step with the Spirit.
—Galatians 5:25 ESV

When I was fourteen, I started playing club volleyball, and I was on San Diego Volleyball Club's worst fourteen-year-old team, 14-Green. 14-Blue was elite, 14-Red was almost elite, and 14-White was really good.

Then there were all seven of us on 14-Green. Beginners.

Deanna, a college volleyball player at San Diego State, was our coach. She would often bring her very cute boyfriend, Tag, to our practices—which was one part thrilling and one part embarrassing (because we were so bad)—and he would try to help us too.

Deanna was very blonde and very tan and she wore *Quelques Fleurs* perfume that would fill the gym as practice would go on.

She was kind of a goddess to me. You know, *that girl*. She was the person who taught me how to hit a volleyball. The right way.

Over the course of my time on 14-Green, we practiced learning the proper approach and timing and technique to hit a volleyball. And I was awful.

I grew up watching my older sister, Laura, play. I watched countless girls approach and hit the volleyball. Left, right, left. Jump. Swing.

But as you might imagine, it's a lot harder than it looks. And when it was my turn to learn the finer points of being a hitter, it took time. A long time. An entire club season, in fact.

Each week at practice Deanna would set so we had perfect sets and we'd practice over and over and over again. Getting the rhythm and the timing and the footwork and the swing. It's a complicated thing, jumping and hitting a ball that's also moving.

Here's the reality: you don't get it until you finally get it. You lumber awkwardly. You miss the ball altogether, maybe. You trip over your own two feet. You send the ball sailing off your wrist, floating out of bounds, because you haven't learned how to put topspin on the ball yet. You get too far under the ball, or behind it, or ahead of it. You hit the net because you haven't yet figured out your body in the air. You look as awkward as a fourteen-year-old girl could look, which is miserable.

On the second-to-last practice for 14-Green, I approached—left, right, left—jumped, reached up, and I hit the ball out of the air and I knew THAT was what it was supposed to feel like to hit a volleyball. THAT was it.

Something clicked.

But it wouldn't have clicked without a year's worth of showing up. Not for me anyway. That's the inconvenient truth.

A couple of months later, I made the varsity volleyball team at my high school as a freshman, played throughout high school, and went on to play in college. I was never an Olympian or anything, but I played and I was actually decent and I always loved it.

Years ago, I attended a lecture about ancient spiritual practices. I spent the entire hour dumbstruck, like I had happened onto the newest information I had ever heard, which was total irony because the word *ancient* was literally in the title of the lecture. I was struck by the idea of seeing my faith journey as a "practice," as opposed to, I don't know, a theory. Sure, I had been in church services my entire life and understood the concepts of prayer, worship, and sacraments, but it wasn't until I sat through this inspiring lecture that I began to understand the significance and sacredness of learning to practice my faith. I wanted to develop a personal practice that included disciplines that were meaningful to me.

To practice means to learn by repeated performance. It is an ongoing pursuit, a habit, a routine. Our practice puts legs to our faith, taking it from something we're reading about or talking about or learning about to something we are participating in, something we are involved in crafting with God. Practicing is learning to encounter, over and over again. Our practices can be conventional, taken from the monks. Or they can be ultimately creative, a confluence of our soul language and God's presence.

We practice in order to get the rhythm of our soul. We practice to return to the song of eternity that we, during certain seasons of life, lose the words to or can't hear anymore. The practice reteaches us the steps. It reminds us that we are marked with eternity, and so we need to touch eternity every so often. This, to me, is the definition of worship.

We hide behind answers, information, our sense of knowing. Engaging in a practice creates vulnerability. We have to drop our defensive knowing and allow life to begin again in the very moment we are living.

The first line of the preface of the *Book of Common Prayer* reads, "It is a most invaluable part of that blessed 'liberty wherewith Christ has made us free,' that in his worship different forms and usages may without offence be allowed."

Your practice could include a variety of things. You have freedom! Prayer practices, time in nature, spiritual direction, journaling, art. When your practice includes time in Scripture, your interaction with the Word should be from a posture of inspiration, not information. Our practices allow the words to live and breathe presently. Sometimes this requires taking the absolute tiniest nibbles—one phrase at a time—and really savoring those bites instead of conquering large swaths without connection.

Your practice might include regular beauty intake from your favorite store. Or regularly scheduled time with other women you trust. Maybe it's yoga on the beach. Or going to a baseball game. You could commit to a regular walk. Maybe laundry is part of your practice, and you use that time to pray while your hands move. Your practice might include waking up an hour earlier every morning and spending the time stretching, moving, breathing, listening. Maybe you need long drives and loud music. Maybe you create a small corner of your home or bedroom that becomes a sanctuary for you.

The key is engagement, ritualistic engagement. The key is remembering how important it is to show up for practice every day. We learn the steps—we keep in step[1]—from practicing. Where do you see beauty? Where do you see God? What is your soul longing to see, taste, touch?

As you might imagine, practice is so incredibly easy to show up for when you are the best player on the team, when you are on your game. Practice is much more intimidating when you're stumbling, fumbling, trying to find your timing and your footwork.

I think it's actually subversive to the darkness when we choose to walk ourselves out into the light each and every day, however awkwardly. We fight back with twenty minutes of soul time. We put on our running shoes or get out our paints. We move our bodies and our hands. We take a long bath. We call the therapist. We schedule a sitter. We sit on the floor and play. We turn toward our spouse. We forgive. We buy ourselves the good candle at Anthro (and we light it).

I believe taking some time to develop a practice when it comes to your faith is time well spent. You and I are, after all, pilgrims, and we are only journeying so long as we are practicing.

Left, right, left.

Reflection & Expression

Consider a few elements of your faith practice. What are some activities, outings, or rituals that would be spiritually significant to you?

For Your Brazen Board

Add an image of something you'd like to include in your faith practice.

34

Welcome It All

The soul should always stand ajar.
—Emily Dickinson

I'm sitting on the floor in my new ~~shed~~ studio. Elaine bought me this gorgeous fuchsia rug for the cement floor. My grandmother's garden chair is in here, as is the aqua coffin cabinet that had the dried bougainvillea bloom stowed away from Bahrain.

I've made this place into a creative space, and a sacred space too. In that way it has become part of my practice. Like an altar in the world, to borrow a line from Barbara Brown Taylor.

I'm practicing the Welcoming Prayer today, a beautiful prayer that opens your hands and your heart and your body and your mind to the very thing you want to ignore, reject, repress. You literally welcome the feeling you want to avoid and ask God to help you sit with that feeling. The idea is that sitting with it, welcoming it in, helps reduce its power. Of course we always believe the opposite—that ignoring something will help it go away.

Haven't you noticed with things like longings, let's say, there's a persistence to the craving that usually won't just skulk off when told? We have to bring them closer instead of send them away.

Father Thomas Keating, a Trappist monk who has dedicated his life to contemplative prayer, gives us these words for the welcoming prayer:

> Welcome, welcome, welcome. I welcome everything that comes to me today because I know it's for my healing. I welcome all thoughts, feelings, emotions, persons, situations, and conditions. I let go of my desire for power and control. I let go of my desire for affection, esteem, approval and pleasure. I let go of my desire for survival and security. I let go of my desire to change any situation, condition, person or myself. I open to the love and presence of God and God's action within. Amen.[1]

I love these lines, this concept, this practice. The Welcoming Prayer takes us out of our heads and into a space where we stop, even for a very few minutes, our analyzing and figuring. We relinquish our strategies and allow God to work within us, in the place where we are far more malleable than our mind. We are opening ourselves up to a divine encounter, which is never a bad idea.

It's not just for those uncomfortable feelings either. The Welcoming Prayer is a practice for welcoming in something we *want* to own or embrace too. Like freedom.

I picture myself dancing on the beach. I welcome the image of myself. I welcome the feelings that come with it. I welcome myself, fully free. I welcome an image of myself walking with God in the lush garden, feeling the spaciousness of that moment, realizing the expanse of his lavishness and creativity.

After these few moments of imagining and welcoming, I blow out the candle and stand up and head back into the house. I am learning to welcome the Crock-Pot and the laundry and the junk mail too. Honoring my everyday skin and honoring my eternal soul, saying to all of it, *You're welcome.*

Reflection & Expression

In your next twenty minutes of soul time, practice the Welcoming Prayer.

What do you need to welcome that you don't want to?

What do you need to welcome that you want more of?

For Your Brazen Board

Find a word or image inspired by your own welcoming prayer. Or take a line from Father Keating's prayer and add it.

35

Shake It Off

It's OK not to be OK.

—Unknown

An impala gets chased around the savanna by a hungry lion. It narrowly escapes with its life, and do you know what it does once it's safe?

It shakes. It shakes out the panic of having to run for its life. Its body physiologically rids itself of all the trauma by shaking. It does this instinctually. And then, once its body has returned to a steady state, once the impala has shaken out all the fight or flight chemicals racing through its body, it goes on. Finds something to eat. Meets up with a friend. What have you. But not until it's done shaking. Only then can it function as usual.

Well, this really makes some sense when you think about it.

When I get panicked or worried, my hands shake, my voice shakes, my knees shake. My body is responding to the

202

overwhelming experience. My hormones are shifting. The chemical balance of my brain is changing. My body is reacting. Doesn't it make sense that I may need to spend some time shaking all that off? But do I? Do I really take the time to shake? Do you? Or are we right back to business as usual? Moving on?

Trauma has a way of piling up and burying us alive—one stressful, hypervigilant situation after another can absolutely destroy our aliveness and awakeness. Not that I have any experience with this whatsoever, of course.

The other night I had a dream kangaroos were chasing me through a building like an apartment complex or hotel. I would run to a room and slam the door behind me and they'd pound on the door trying to get at me and punch me. Then I'd narrowly escape and run to another room and as soon as I'd get the door closed they'd be pounding on it again, trying to get in and beat me up. And so on, for like a hundred years.

I don't know if you've ever been chased by a crew of hostile kangaroos in real life or in a dream, but it's no joke.

The next morning I looked up the significance of kangaroos in dreams. This kind of thing always fascinates me. I read the following online: "To dream of being chased by a kangaroo may represent a wish to avoid having to do something the hard way. Not wanting to take the long route in a situation. Doing everything you can to avoid facing a more difficult method of dealing with something. Avoiding a protracted dilemma, or needless difficulty."[1]

Who me?

I counted how many times the word *avoid* was used in that description and I wanted to crawl under the bed. Sure, OK, you got me. I'd prefer to avoid. Namely, my humanity. My limits. My mental health. My need to stop and shake. Having to "do things the hard way." It's all so terribly inconvenient.

If we refuse to shake, though, the kangaroo comes for us. It's inevitable.

Steve and I had to shake off our time overseas. We did this well some days—intentionally recovering—and we did this poorly some days—intentionally numbing. We brought in the borders of our life so that we could begin to breathe again. It kinda sucked for about a year and a half. And then we had a party on the Fourth of July.

Independence Day.

We had Eric and Kara and two of their girls in town for the weekend and a houseful of adults and kids. Steve grilled carne asada and pollo asado and everyone brought a special something from their own kitchen to share. Audi's jalapeno cream sauce was *the* hit. I literally wanted to bathe in it.

At one point in the afternoon, all the dads were in the pool with the kids—raucous and rowdy—while all the moms huddled together to catch up. And then at another point in the afternoon all the dads were circled up under the big market umbrella, some reclining on lounge chairs, one rocking his baby girl in his arms, while the moms were all in the hot tub passing around the toddlers as we talked and laughed. We gave the kids sparklers, and they were all terrified and cried, which is just what a party is like with a lot of littles. We roasted s'mores on the back patio around the fire pit. We covered every inch of our house and our yard. I looked up at some point in the evening, and kids were perched on the boulders outside our kitchen windows, talking and laughing and helping the little ones scramble up. Like kid-reptiles, sunning and scurrying.

I don't have a single picture of the day to show you, which is evidence that I either had no idea where my phone was for most of the day or that I didn't care.

Previously, Steve and I had been in a season of recovery. We needed a season of reduction, where we turned inward and we rested and healed and took intentional care of ourselves. A season of slow and simple. A season to shake.

And on the Fourth, I felt this deep satisfaction from opening wide the doors of our house and welcoming in a troupe of friends and their darlings. I actually felt moved and teary as I stood back and surveyed the whole scene.

If you're in a shaky season, I can relate more than you know. The best thing you can do for yourself is let it out. Take your time and let it all out. Rest, refuel, take in a whole lot of beauty, do whatever it takes to breathe, accept your limits. One day, after six months or a year—or almost eighteen months in our case—your capacity will return incrementally. You'll be ready to experiment with a bit of expansion. You will open the doors, and it will feel so good.

But first, shake.

Reflection & Expression

What would it look like for you to shake?

For Your Brazen Board

Add an image that represents rest to you.

Add the words "Don't forget to shake."

36

Break at Least One Rule

The mind I love must have wild places.
—Katherine Mansfield

Bear Bryant, the legendary coach of the University of Alabama Crimson Tide, allegedly once told the media that there are two kinds of football players who are no good: "The ones who never do anything you tell them, and the ones who always do everything you tell them."

My dad told me that story last summer. I'm still thinking about it.

So many of us have lived our lives by a series of rules, the kind of rules that others told us would make us good, successful, loved. The kind of rules that would keep everyone comfortable. We were shown these rules in a thousand different ways, re-inforced by a thousand different experiences of embarrassment, praise, discomfort, acceptance. The rules were taught and they were caught.

If we wake up one day and realize we don't really know what we want or what we think about things, doesn't that mean—perhaps—the rules didn't serve us?

Breaking rules for the sake of breaking rules is adolescent. But is there an outside chance you're following rules that are contributing to your hiding?

Is that possible?

Here are six rules you may be following (without even knowing it, in some cases) that will not serve you. I only tell you this because I've learned the hard way.

Rule #1: You must tame your husband.

I'm probably going to get into some hot water here, but I have witnessed time and time again this pervasive cancer of we women wanting to emasculate our husbands and then getting diabolically contemptuous when they become passive and detached.

My husband does and says a lot of stuff that makes me uncomfortable. Some of which we're working through and some of which I need to just let go of. I need to let him nurture his own wild so I can honor and enjoy the very best parts of him. This is tricky, messy, totally uncharted, and therapy-worthy. The Soul Bullies want to give us a list of rules we must abide by and our loved ones must abide by too, no matter their interests, personalities, or preferences. This is because the Soul Bullies are all about control. Would I rather control my husband or know him? (Depends on the day, to be honest.)

For many years of our marriage, I believed all of Steve's behavior reflected back on me, which made me take way too much responsibility for him. The experts call this enmeshment, I think. Or is it codependence? Either way, I've had to learn to back away, get my grubby little hands off of his life, and let him sink or swim on his own. Great practice for raising kids too. Ugghhh.

Steve is going to hunt animals and cook them and eat them. Steve is going to cuss. Steve is going to talk about politics a little too aggressively. Steve is going to do a whole host of things I would prefer to edit and domesticate. But here is the down-and-dirty truth: I have never gained anything by trying to get Steve to be the version of himself that would make me most comfortable. Period.

To tell you the truth, the thing I am drawn to most in Steve is this wild. I often wonder if so much of what I'm attracted to in him are the things I long to be. So much of who Steve is are the very things that are locked way down in my soul, nudging for release. He's not really all that worried about trying to win people over. He loves the people he loves fiercely. He doesn't need your approval. I think people are drawn to these things in him. I know I am.

I want Steve to be the version of himself that celebrates his soul. (Even if I have to turn around and walk away and breathe deeply.) And I want him to do the same for me.

Rule #2: You must avoid pleasure.

Pleasure is one of those words with a lot of baggage, an idea we've gotten really wrong. I don't have it the least bit figured out. Most of us either indulge or deprive, and we do not know how to experience pleasure in a way that is God-designed. We're either chasing the forbidden or we're flatlined.

I want a greater capacity to experience pleasure and to do so appropriately. I want to enjoy food without overindulging.

I want to enjoy alcohol moderately. I want to love clothes and home décor without becoming a hoarder. I want to experience sex more intimately and profoundly. I want to see beauty in the beige and the back alley, and let that beauty sink into my soul in a way that brings me endless pleasure. Like the pomegranates. I want to believe I was made for pleasure instead of being wary of experiencing gratification.

I don't want to binge on pleasure, which is actually about numbing instead of feeling. I don't want to repress or demonize pleasure, either, which is also about numbing instead of feeling.

I want to give myself permission to savor the garden of experiences God's given us. Long meals. Deep breaths. Slow sips. Soft skin. And in the places where I am blocked and bruised and binging, I want the courage to seek out help and healing.

Rule #3: You must put yourself last.

I believe in the value of servanthood. I believe in self-sacrificing love. I believe in putting my own needs aside to take care of those I have vowed, before God, to take care of. However, I do not like any sentiment that constantly reinforces the idea that my needs are *less* important than my husband's and my children's and my home's and my pet's and my boss's. I don't think this line of thinking helps anyone.

For example, how many times a day do you need to pee and you don't? You simply don't go because you don't have time, don't consider your body's basic functions a priority.

I spoke at a women's event at Christmas and I gave them a whole list of helpful suggestions, if I do say so myself. I talked about creating breathing room during the busy holiday bustle and happened to mention that one of the ways they could honor themselves this season was by listening to their bodies a bit more intuitively—sleep when they need to sleep, eat when they need to eat, pee when they need to pee, and so on.

I had a line of women waiting to talk to me after. Do you know what they all wanted to discuss (THROUGH TEARS)? They all wanted to tell me how they constantly dance around their lives—one more load of laundry, one more lunch packed, one more email, one more meeting—because they have to pee. And it's making them frantic.

Do you know what my husband does when he has to pee? He walks down the hall to the bathroom and he pees. Do you know what I do and so many of my friends do when we have to pee? We hold it. Until we're in pain and panicked. We are crazy people. Even animals don't do this.

Step One: Go Pee.

Rule #4: You must be available to everyone all the time.

I don't have voice mail set up on my phone. I haven't for the last two years. When we lived overseas, voice mail was not an option, and Steve and I got used to communicating by call or text and not having to leave messages on people's phones.

When we returned from living overseas the first time in 2004, I did set up voice mail on my phone, and I found myself drowning in the various communication streams I needed to check. I couldn't keep up. Within a couple of days, my voice mail space would fill up and I'd have twenty or so messages to listen to and calls to return and then people would call or text or email to tell me that my voice mail was full and they couldn't leave a message. I thought I was going to hurt someone.

I never really considered the fact that I could just shut it down. No one was forcing me to be available to everyone all the time through every means possible.

I am not saying it is sinful to have voice mail. Seriously, I'm not. I'm simply telling you that I currently don't have the capacity for any more contact.

So when we returned from living overseas the second time, Steve and I both decided there'd be nothing wrong with never setting up our voice mail. Sure, I think it likely annoys the heck out of my mom and mother-in-law. Caller ID tells me I missed a call from a doctor's office and I have to return the call. But overall, it's so nice to have one less thing I need to check.

Most of all, no voice mail is one small YES to my mental health even if it means people are going to say things like, "Did you know you don't have your voice mail set up? I can show you how to do that if you need some help. It's really simple. And that way people can get in touch with you whenever they need to."

Got it. Thanks.

Rule #5: You must listen to the experts.

I love the show *Project Runway*. I love it mainly because I am so intrigued by people's creative process, especially their intuition as it relates to their individual voice. These designers get huge challenges with tiny time frames and they are asked to pull off a miracle, episode after episode. Season after season, the successful designers say much the same thing: "There isn't time to second-guess yourself. You have to trust your gut, trust your aesthetic, and go for it."

In a recent season the designer's mentor, Tim Gunn, kept giving a designer named Char pointed advice about her design concepts, often trying to convince her to go in a different direction with her work. She would always politely listen to him, and then she'd stick with her original plan, one time saying, "Tim, sometimes you gotta leave a little room for the magic."

I didn't always love what Char made, but I've never forgotten that line. The "experts" will always have ideas, conventional wisdom, and advice for us. Usually this input is given with the best intentions. But sometimes we need to trust our own gut, our own voice, that nudge in our spirit, and we need to leave a little room for the magic (the magic that, just maybe, only we can see).

How many times have you been told, "Just listen to the people who know best"? Others' experiences have merits, sure. But so do our own attempts, false starts, intuitions, visions. We need to start believing we are a reliable source in the world. Everyone else does not always know better. Your observations are valid.

Bear Bryant had it right: we can't always do everything we're told, and we better not be the kind of people who never do anything we're told.

In other words: Don't be a punk. And don't be a pleaser. Learn, instead, to be a poet.

Rule #6: You must consider your body a liability.

So many of us were told—and this is still being preached— that if girls wouldn't act and dress in certain ways, then boys wouldn't have to be so naughty. We were responsible for their choices, their thoughts, their addictions, even. This is so significantly crappy.

Many of the young women receiving this message, internalizing this message, realized they needed to shut off some essential things about themselves if they were going to survive in a culture of "keeping the boys clean."

What's so very sad about all this is that we heard the message OVER and OVER again that the boys' sobriety was far more important and to be protected than the girls' sexuality.

We have women who have been told their entire lives that being a woman is a liability. And what follows, then, is women who now believe their bodies are liabilities too.

How do women who have internalized these messages have an exciting, free sex life? How in the world could these women ever in a million years make amends with their bodies? I recently attended a half-day event all on the topic of sex. I was reminded what a treacherous subject this is, how deeply so many are wounded, and how carefully we must tread when it comes to talking about sex, bodies, pornography, sexual abuse, marital disharmony, and marital satisfaction. We are in the midst of untold brokenness. Ours and everyone else's.

One of the women at this event told her story: She and her husband were the model of Christian marriage. And then seven years into their marriage, he admitted his sex addiction and their lives came crashing down.

Now, over twenty years since his confession, you can see that this couple has been through hell and back and they've fought for what they have. She told us about the shame she felt, how viscerally shameful she felt for years, and the one thing that helped:

She gave each of us a blank 3x5 card and had us paraphrase Psalm 34:5 on it with our name substituted. It read: *Leeana who looks to the Lord is radiant; Leeana's face is never covered with shame.*

But she didn't stop there. She told us to put our fingers in our ears and to repeat, out loud so that we could hear only our own voice in our head, the sentences. She had us do this over and over again, repeating that we were radiant and without shame. Reading the words with our fingers stuck in our ears. Louder and louder and louder.

She told us she would yell these words twenty or thirty times a day when she was in the marital valley of the shadow of death, believing the toxic lie that her husband would have never looked at other women's bodies if hers had only been enough.

In a recent twenty minutes of soul time, God said to me, "Leeana, now is the time to take exceptional care of your body." And do you know what? I've started realizing how easy it is for me to fall into rhythms of taking hideous care of my body. Do we know how to really feed ourselves nourishing food? Do we know what it means to be hungry and full? Do we know how to take care of our skin? Do we know how to exercise in a way that is strengthening and not bullying? Do we wash our hair? Do we shave our legs? Do we invest time and energy in the proper care and feeding of this one body we've been given?

Perhaps it is time for you, too, to begin taking exceptional care of your body: nourishing it, moving it, feeding it, honoring it.

These are just six rules I think you should consider breaking. I'm sure you've lived by and been burned by many more. Crap like, "You must never let them see you cry," "You must be perfect or you are a failure," and "You must gauge your success in life by the effectiveness of your home décor."

Breaking rules for the sake of breaking rules won't help you feel alive. Many boundaries in life contribute to our freedom, not threaten it. But I also fear for this entire culture of women who can recite the rules but cannot recognize themselves.

Reflection & Expression

What is one rule you need to break?

When was a time you didn't listen and it ended up being a good decision?

For Your Brazen Board

Add an image or symbol of someone breaking the rules for the right reasons.

37

Be the Mess

Then Jesus made a circuit of all the towns and villages.
He taught in their meeting places, reported kingdom news,
and healed their diseased bodies, healed their bruised and
hurt lives. When he looked out over the crowds, his heart
broke. So confused and aimless they were, like sheep with
no shepherd.

—Matthew 9:35–38 Message

A few weeks ago my entire family had some form of the stomach
flu. Lane and I had it the worst; we looked green for seven full
days. This is one of my absolute least favorite ways of being
sick, and the only thing that makes me feel better and helps
me keep my sense of humor is remembering Emily's line from
The Devil Wears Prada: "I'm just one stomach flu away from
my goal weight."

At one point—while in the throes of this horrible bug—I
was in the pick-up line at Luke and Lane's school. Elle was in

her car seat, now fully recovered from her bug. (PS: What is worse than being sick when your kids are well? It's just cosmically unfair.) Lane was in her car seat, throwing up into a bowl I had provided. And we were waiting for Luke, who was now recovered, to come out of class so we could scoop him up, race to Rite Aid for supplies, and get home before I threw up.

Luke and Lane started kindergarten at a school where we didn't know many people, but I have been given the unexpected gift of new friends whom I adore. Literal angels. One of them pulled up next to me in the pick-up line and asked how we were all doing. I rolled my window down just as Lane threw up into her bowl. My friend heard the whole thing.

Here's the deal: Two times previously that same week I had caught this friend as she was taking her son into school and asked her if she could run one or both of my kids in as well. I just couldn't get out of the car. And she gladly did, as I would have done for her without a second thought.

So when she pulled up beside me and we both rolled our windows down to the sound of Lane throwing up, she looked at me and said, "What do you need?" And I deflected. I said, "Oh, we're OK. I'm just going to pick up Luke and run to Rite Aid to get some PediaSure and Pepto. It will be fine." (Lane wretches behind me.)

"Leeana," she said somewhat sternly, "I will go to Rite Aid and bring everything to your house."

"No, no, no," I said. This friend has a brood of her own and I knew it would be a lot for her to pull off an after-school errand with all of her littles in tow. Besides, I hadn't done any favors for her. We were new-ish friends. It would all be too much.

Then she leaned over her passenger seat and said to me slowly, "Leeana, will you let me help you?"

And all my protective edges turned liquid.

"Yes," I said. "Yes, I will let you help me." My shoulders dropped.

I am spoiled rotten when it comes to gorgeous women in my life. Absolutely inundated with extraordinary beauties. But if I'm unwilling to let them in, let them see me in need, if I'm unwilling to create interdependence, then I will never experience the fullness of the relationship.

I don't know why I do this. Maybe I am intolerant of my own need, and I believe these friends will be too. Maybe I don't want to let them see how chaotic my life is, or feels, sometimes. Maybe I'm afraid of being burdensome and annoying.

Years ago, I became friends with two people who were dealing with homelessness, addiction, mental illness, and gender identity issues. They were typically in some sort of crisis. They were also fairly unaware of the social norms that keep order in church offices, so, generally speaking, they caused discomfort when people saw them coming because they were the epitome of needy.

I would simply sit and talk with them . . . often. We talked about drugs and money and mental illness and partners and family and Section 8 housing and abuse and God. We talked about pornography and prayer and doctors and "the system" and bus fare. We talked about fathers and mothers and rejection and Jesus and whether or not I believed it was appropriate to be a Christian and get your fortune read. We talked about the male ego and aggression and therapy and lipstick and AIDS.

At some point in our conversations, I'd have to excuse myself, letting them know I needed to move on with my day. They would always ask me to pray for them, and so we'd end our meetings with prayer. I'd pray for them, and they would pray for me. They'd hug me and tell me they loved me and then they'd walk down to the bus stop. They were relentless and emotionally grabby. They were a certified mess so much of the time, the kind of mess you're glad you aren't, if you know what I mean.

Here's what I know: It's much easier to be the person behind the desk than the person with all the issues. It's much easier to be the helping-out mom than the one in the pick-up line with the stomach flu. It's much easier to be sitting across from the mess, praying for the mess, than to *be* the mess. And what I realize when I try to differentiate myself from the mess is, inevitably, I am the mess too.

When I got pregnant with Luke and Lane, the same two friends from church brought me a little gift one Sunday: a stuffed mama and baby monkey. The mama's arms have Velcro that fasten around the baby and hold it to her. I have no idea where they got the money for this little twosome.

The other day I came across the pair of monkeys, holding on to each other, when I was cleaning up the girls' room. I've never been able to get rid of them. When I picked up the monkeys, I thought about the hours I spent with my two church friends and how unapologetic they were about their need. Almost childlike in their quest for care.

I wondered, even as I was stacking pull-ups and shelving Fancy Nancy books, why I spent so much time with them, opened my door to them over and over again. I think of them with great compassion, something I did not have much of for myself at that season of life.

If we're honest, I don't think any of us would say we feel particularly tolerant of our own neediness. In fact, if I'm honest, I have to confess I can be downright contemptuous of this naked part of me. How dare I need rescue? How dare I need saving? How dare I appear helpless? I buy into the lie that it's far more brazen to appear fixed, and so I must pack on a plastered periphery so no one sees the needy me. *The needy me is unpredictable and inconvenient,* I think. *No one will like her.*

Maybe the time I spent sitting with those friends from church was about growing increasingly comfortable with the need in someone else so that I might someday be able to feel a bit more comfortable with the need in me.

We don't come out of hiding because of our competence and smooth exteriors—because we've finally got it all together. We come out of hiding because we learn to embrace, with compassion, all the varied nuances of our humanity.

Do not wait to let us see you until you feel you are ready—spit shined and coifed. These moments never come. Let us see you because you are *not* ready. And yet, you have listened to the compassionate voice of God speaking over you and within you and, with courage, you allow him to chip away at the plastered cast around your soul so that we may all get the unique gift of the fleshy you.

Reflection & Expression

Consider the last time you were in need and asked for help.

When was a time you were in need and refused to receive help?

For Your Brazen Board

Add a picture of someone in need. (And maybe it's a picture of you.)

38

Say Goodbye to the Geysers

Whether you turn to the right or to the left, your ears will
hear a voice behind you, saying, "This is the way; walk in it."

—Isaiah 30:21 NIV

The other morning I got the kids settled at school and ran
back home to get changed for a speaking engagement, only to
find a sprinkler had erupted and a geyser was gushing behind
our garage.

Wouldn't you know it, on that one day a week when I shower.

It was the worst possible timing for something like this to
happen, which is just so like life . . . the unfortunate event dis-
rupts us and delays us and derails us when we are in our favorite
shoes and we finally got our hair done.

I arrived at the event feeling a little teetery and tottery, and
the Soul Bullies were having their usual heyday. When my day
takes a turn for the worse is often when the bullies are at their
harrowing best.

This is what you might call a perfect storm, the kind of disruption that turns into far more than a shooting stream of water in the yard. Somehow, this sprinkler leak becomes the evidence that you are on an entirely wrong and completely misguided path in your life. What was, at first, a maintenance issue is now a metaphor. Your life is out of control. Your life is one giant mudslide of a mess.

And, without totally realizing what we've done, we give in to the geysers. We say, "You're right. What was I *thinking*? Walking out into the world, showing up today, is a bad idea. Dabbling is insane. Creating is nuts. Using my voice is a liability. I'm going to just go back in the house and rehearse how the universe is conspiring against me."

Do you know what the geysers are? They are distractions. They are the way the dark forces of this world try to keep the gorgeous thing from being born. Not annihilation; just simply distraction. If these distracting forces can shift our focus from soul-tending to mini-crisis, they know we're off the scent.

What geyser in your life is going off—histrionically waving its obnoxious hands—trying to get you to tend to it instead of what you really need to be working on? "Over here!" it yells. "Over here! Look at me!" The geyser's only aim is to divert you just long enough to claim your energy, your focus, and your intention.

Man, this makes me angry. Here we are—a minor miracle that we're even clothed and in our right minds—and the geysers are coming for us.

I don't know what geyser is or was gushing at your house today, what you need to overcome in order to stroll through the garden of your soul for a time, but I'm holding out hope that distractions aren't going to win the day. Disruptions won't prevail. That you can walk outside and saunter right past the yet-to-be-dealt-with because you know it's inevitable that mayhem is going to come knocking on your door right about the time you get some things in your soul figured out. And you can chuckle because you've got that geyser's number.

You are not going to allow the mess to make you feel overly responsible for a sprinkler head and under-responsible for your own soul. When it begins whining for your attention, you do what my friend Linsey says to do. You say, "Sorry. This time, I'm choosing me."

Reflection & Expression

What is one distraction in your life right now?

For Your Brazen Board

Add an image that represents you choosing you.

39

A Letter to My Daughters

Just in case you ever foolishly forget, I am never not thinking about you.

—Virginia Woolf

To my girls,

I'm watching you. I'm watching you love and learn and lean into your own brazen ways. I'm watching what makes you laugh and what makes you cry. I'm watching how you move and how you groove. I'm watching you sleep and watching you play. I'm watching.

There will be days, especially in the years ahead, when it might feel like I don't see you at all, like I'm not reading your signals, like we're speaking two different languages. I'm going to mess up. I'm going to make assumptions when I should be listening. I'm going to lose my patience when I should breathe. I'm going to want things for you *that you don't want for yourself. We, too, will endure and enjoy the mysterious complexities of every mother/ daughter relationship that has come before us. But no matter what, I'll be watching.*

I will be paying attention, witnessing, when you are trying to make new friends. When nightmares are coming for you. When your body is changing. When you are out and about with boys. I will be paying attention when you are learning to drive a car. When you are making decisions about your grown-up life. I will be paying attention by watching, praying, asking, holding, hoping, believing, and setting up your highly trained father on surveillance stakeouts. (Just kidding about that last part . . . –ish.)

Most of all, I will hold space for your soul, a watch- man for the Created You, a custodian for your voice . . . because I believe you are already *brazen babes. You are unconditionally complete in every way, and you are so beautifully becoming too. Both of you in your own ways. I get glimpses of your soul, Lane, when you leave notes for me like "You are byootfl" and "God job Mommy" and "Be brav. God keps us saf," when I see how truly pro- lific and generous you are with your ideas and creations, and when I see you sitting up tall on a horse. And I get glimpses of your soul, Elle, when you sidle up to me and say, "Hi, Mommy Delicious" and when you call Daddy every morning after he leaves for work and you hug the phone while you talk to him and when—at not even two years old—you started jumping off the diving board like it was your job.*

Hopefully I will help you confront the not-worth-your- time voices—the toxic ones in our heads, the mean girls, the preying boys, the curtailers and the controllers and those who would rather you keep it down, please, if you don't mind.

Hopefully, I will show you—with my actions more than words—what it means to live from God's wild love and to return to him again and again, to find him in the cool of the morning and the twilight of the evening, and to allow myself to be found by him too. Hopefully I will teach you how to scout beauty, to be filled up and inspired, and to let the loveliness of God himself nourish you.

I want the courage to mother you brazenly—to mother you from a place deeper than shame and fear. I want you to grow up never questioning your beauty, your wonder. I want you to be surrounded by women who stoke—instead of tame—your wild. "The world needs more of you, Lane and Elle, not less of you," they will say. A big part of your journey will be believing them.

Make a habit out of surrounding yourself with women who have felt the freedom to become, women who are embracing their wounds and their wonder, women who are journeying. Make a habit out of surrounding yourself with women who need you to be bigger, not smaller. And make a habit out of surrounding yourself with women who are available to love you.

These are the brazen ladies. They will save you. You will save each other. You will say to each other, over and over:

"You are that girl."

"No, you are."

Reflection & Expression

Write a letter to someone you love, encouraging them to be brazen.

For Your Brazen Board

If it's not there already, add the word *brazen*.

40

Already

The secret to having it all is believing you already do.
—Unknown

At the end of Paulo Coelho's *The Alchemist*, the boy in the story is planning to return to his love. He has been on the pilgrimage of his Personal Legend. And he has found his treasure. The wind picks up, the levanter wind blowing in from Africa. Carried on the wind is the scent of a familiar perfume, the perfume of the boy's love. And, also, a kiss that finds its way to his mouth. Immediately the boy knows who has sent this scent, this kiss.

"I'm coming, Fatima," the boy says.

And the book ends.

I'm closing this book similarly. With the knowledge that we must fight like warriors for our treasure, we must seek out our voice and our desires and our space in this world, we must turn a listening ear to our longings, all the while knowing love was already there, always there, waiting for us to come home to it. Your Created Center was breathed into existence by God himself, and there is nothing anyone has done to you or anything you've done to yourself that can wreck it.

God has already anchored you in his love. Through Christ, our freedom is secured, and we can return to the garden to dabble in the longings of our hands. We are *both* complete *and* we are becoming, and the great joy of our lives is investigating and living out of both of these truths. Free to rest. Free to run.

Some of the etymology of the word *already* is "from an earlier time." Yes, exactly.

The you that has been hiding has already, always been there. We just have to learn to recognize her rhythms. We have to be willing to abandon the try for the mystery of trust. The journey is less about arriving and more about returning: to the truth we already knew, to the love we already have, to the beauty we already see.

We are always being beckoned home.

Maybe "the treasure" is knowing who we are and where home is and who is waiting for us there. God looks for us in the quiet of the morning. He sends his love on the wind. He calls out to us, "Where are you?"

Our whole life is to be the answer, "I'm coming."

Reflection & Expression

What do you already have?

For Your Brazen Board

At some point, spend some time with your Brazen Board that you've created over the course of this book. Consider what surprised you when you added it. Certainly there will also be elements you added that you already knew were a part of you. Maybe those were forgotten elements re-found, but I would bet there are pictures, textures, colors that have always been a part of your story. They were in you already, and you just needed to go in search of them.

Be absolutely sure to share your Brazen Board with some trusted friends. Talk them through what you've created and why, if you have an inkling. Make sure you spend time thinking and explaining and processing your board.

And my very last request would be to put it in a place in your home or office where you will see it, where it will seep into your being.

You are a Brazen Warrior.

I believe in you.

A Brazen Benediction

I have finished this book on the grounds of St. Gregory's the Great Catholic Church, sitting beside the fountain that runs from the cross, on by the bench where I'm sitting, down to the mouth of the property. Two flowering fuchsia bougainvillea plants just happen to flank me, vines crawling up the columns on my left and on my right. Above me, a heavily patinaed copper dome rises up into the clearest sky—aqua against azure—an embellished gothic cross reaches skyward atop the dome. I watch a bird rest on an arm of the cross. Feel a whisper of a breeze brush by. It's a cool morning, the first break we've had in this late fall heat wave. Dew is on the grass. Every once in a while a leaf falls from the tree canopy above me and hits me right on top of the head.

I'm sharing this space with a statue of St. Gregory the Great, the patron of this church who is best known for his namesake, the Gregorian Chant. He holds a book open, and in his book are written his own words:

> Humbly we bend before the Lord of Light,
> and pray at early dawn,

that this Sweet love may all our sin forgive,
and make our miseries cease;
may grant us health,
and grant us the gift divine of everlasting peace.

Amen.

Acknowledgments

Basically every last thing that happens in my life happens because of what you might call a "team effort." Certainly, book writing is a major example of this phenomenon. Here is the team that put effort into this project . . .

Christopher Ferebee has championed me and this project, and I'm endlessly grateful for his representation, his wisdom, and his belief in me.

Andrea Doering is both a gifted editor and a stalwart supporter. Her keen eye and compassionate direction always make me better. I'm honored to be on her team.

Twila Bennett has invested in me personally and professionally. I'm grateful for her strategic ideas, her ongoing energy, and her willingness to take risks.

I don't take too many steps in life without the companionship, rescue, and loud cheering of My Group. These brazen ladies are Debbie Cressey, Kate Kopp Jackson, Corrie Klekowski, Tatum Lehman, Wanida Maertz, Jamie Rettig, Tina Rose, Erica Ruse, and Joanna Wasmuth. #saved

Kara Jung mailed me a booklet of handwritten promises that have sustained and guided me at many junctures in this project.

I'm grateful for Melinda Miller; Eddy and Becky Miller; Bill and Joanie Tankersley; Lance and Laura Hatfield; Jackson and Lindsay Hatfield; Trey and Elyse Miller; Nathan, Lea, and Bennett Miller; Peter and Jacquline Tankersley; Fynn and Ollie Tankersley. Thank you for your love, care, help, support, jokes, stories, and investment in me and mine.

Elyse Miller provided exceptional editorial feedback in early (and late) drafts of this book. She was a translator and a truth-teller all along the way, and her input had a profound impact on the finished product.

Thank you for the talks on the back patio, Trey.

Thank you for your text, Laura.

The True Beauties at Revell always blow me away with their skill and style. They are Barb Barnes, Jean Bloom, and Brittany Miller.

Timely conversations with Krysta Henningsen and Jolynn Brown in the inception stages of *Brazen* were affirming.

Linsey Wildey walks with me through life in such a way that provides remarkable depth and connectedness. She is a stabilizing force and a spiritual companion, and I'm sure many of our conversations are woven into the fabric of this book.

Beth Slevcove will never know, on this earth anyway, how tenderly she has guided me back to myself and back to God. I don't even really think she's real, to tell you the truth.

Elaine Hamilton and I don't spend all that much time away from each other. This has proved to deepen and clarify the concepts in this book. Additionally, her presence has grounded me, nourished me, lightened me, and entertained me endlessly. In fact, the entire Hamilton clan, including Mr. Ken, Katie, and

Josh, have surrounded us with so many of life's essentials: food, drink, laughter, and childcare. We are so lucky.

Luke, Lane, and Elle are the richest joys of my life. To know them, to love and to raise them is my greatest privilege and contribution to this world. They are so delicious.

I do not know a more brazen human being than my Stevie T. His perseverance, strength, intensity, humor, and clarity are endlessly intriguing to me. I am entirely grateful for the ways he clears the path so I can do this work.

Notes

Chapter 1 Honor Your Created Center

1. Michael Phillips, *A God to Call Father* (Wheaton: Tyndale, 1994).
2. Ecclesiastes 3:11.
3. While this quote is often attributed to Maya Angelou, some sources cite Angelou as quoting the poet James Baldwin.

Chapter 2 Emerge from the Beige

1. C. S. Lewis, *Till We Have Faces* (New York: Harcourt, Brace and Co., 1956), 294.
2. Eep Crood of the movie *The Croods*.

Chapter 3 Take Twenty Minutes of Soul Time

1. See Matthew 11:29–30.
2. See Matthew 11:28–30.

Chapter 5 Unhook from Heavy

1. Psalm 90:17 Message.
2. John 14:27 Message, emphasis added.
3. See John 15:4–5 Message.
4. See Psalm 32:7.

Chapter 6 Keep Casting Your Nets

1. My riff on Galatians 6:9.
2. 2 Samuel 24:24, paraphrased.

Chapter 7 See the Pepper Tree

1. Kathleen Norris, *Acedia & Me* (New York: Riverhead, 2008), 230.

Chapter 8 Looking through the Divine View-Master

1. Mary Pipher, *Reviving Ophelia: Saving the Selves of Adolescent Girls* (New York: Penguin, 2005), 159.

Chapter 9 Seek and Find

1. Lauren F. Winner, *Wearing God* (New York: HarperOne, 2015). 2–3.
2. See Isaiah 30:18.
3. See Psalm 105.

Chapter 11 Allow for Expansion

1. Irwin Kula, *Yearnings: Embracing the Sacred Messiness of Life* (New York: Hyperion, 2006).

Chapter 12 Replace the Fig Leaves

1. David Benner, *The Gift of Being Yourself* (Downers Grove, IL: InterVarsity, 2004), 83.

Chapter 13 Fall in Love

1. "Frivolous." *Merriam-Webster.com*. Merriam-Webster, http://www.merriam-webster.com/dictionary/frivolous.

2. "Frivolous," Online Etymology Dictionary, http://www.etymonline.com/index.php?term=frivolous.

Chapter 18 Make Peace with Self-Possession

1. Margery Williams, *The Velveteen Rabbit* (New York: Doubleday, 1922), 5.

Chapter 20 Commemorate the Clarity

1. See Joshua 4:1–24.

Chapter 21 Disobey Your Fear

1. Henry Cloud, *Integrity* (New York: HarperCollins, 2006), subtitle.

2. See James 1:5.

3. "Fearless," NPR.com, http://www.npr.org/programs/invisibilia/377515477/fearless.

4. Ibid.

Chapter 22 Explore Dimensionally

1. See Hebrews 11:13–16.

Chapter 25 Watch for Rescue

1. 1 Samuel 17:47, paraphrased.

Chapter 26 Curate Your Life

1. Another resource that's been very helpful is Gabrielle Stanley Blair's *Design Mom: How to Live with Kids: A Room-by-Room Guide*. She discusses every room in a family home, including entryways, laundry areas, closets, and all the other little nooks and crannies that go into the workability of a home. She certainly addresses the major rooms and how she conceptualizes their purposefulness, but she also emphasizes the small spaces that either help our homes work or get in the way of the dailyness of living with lots of hands and feet in one house. Her suggestions have really helped me think through what is and isn't working in our home and where I might allocate resources to create a bit more functionality. All in the name of keeping every one of the five Tanks in our household a bit more sane.

Chapter 28 Risk like Rowan and Rousey

1. "A Message to Garcia" by Elbert Hubbard first appeared in *The Philistine* in 1899. It has been printed and reprinted more than any other piece of literature in the history of the world, except the Bible.

2. Tama Kieves, *This Time I Dance!* (New York: Penguin, 2002).

3. Theodore Roosevelt, "The Man in the Arena." Excerpt from the speech "Citizenship in a Republic" delivered at the Sorbonne, in Paris, France, on 23 April 1910; http://www.theodore-roosevelt.com/trsorbonnespeech.html.

Chapter 29 Drop the Drapes

1. Sue Monk Kidd and Ann Kidd Taylor, *Traveling with Pomegranates* (New York: Viking, 2009).

Chapter 33 Develop a Practice

1. See Galatians 5:25.

Chapter 34 Welcome It All

1. Thomas Keating, *Open Mind, Open Heart* (Warwick, NY: Amity House, 1986).

Chapter 35 Shake It Off

1. Read more at: http://www.mydreamvisions.com/dreamdictionary/symbol/1814/Copyright2013MyDreamVisions.com.

Leeana Tankersley is the author of *Found Art* and *Breathing Room* and holds English degrees from Liberty University and West Virginia University. She and her husband, Steve, live in San Diego, California, with their three babies: Luke (7), Lane (7), and Elle (4). Leeana writes about living from the spacious place and beginning again on her blog, www.leeanatankersley.com.

Instagram: @lmtankersley
Twitter: @lmtankersley
Facebook: www.facebook.com/tankersleyleeana

"Leeana says out loud the things we all feel, and she says it with grace and eloquence. Reading these pages is like sitting with a friend."

—*Shauna Niequist,* author of *Bread & Wine*

CONNECT WITH

Leeana Tankersley

at LeeanaTankersley.com

f tankersleyleeana

🐦 lmtankersley

📷 lmtankersley